Trucks, Planes and Cars coloring book

This book belong to

. . . .

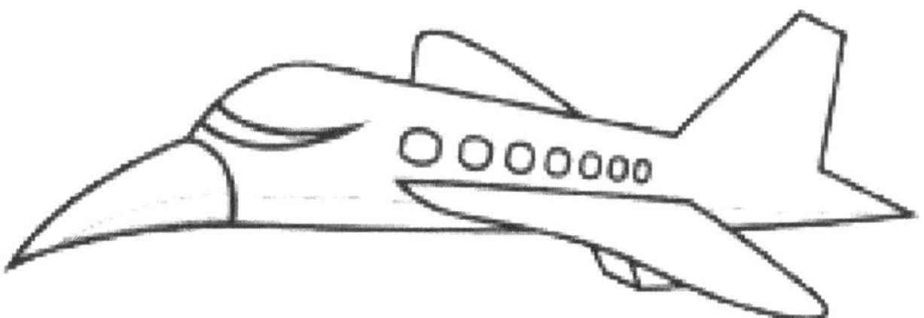

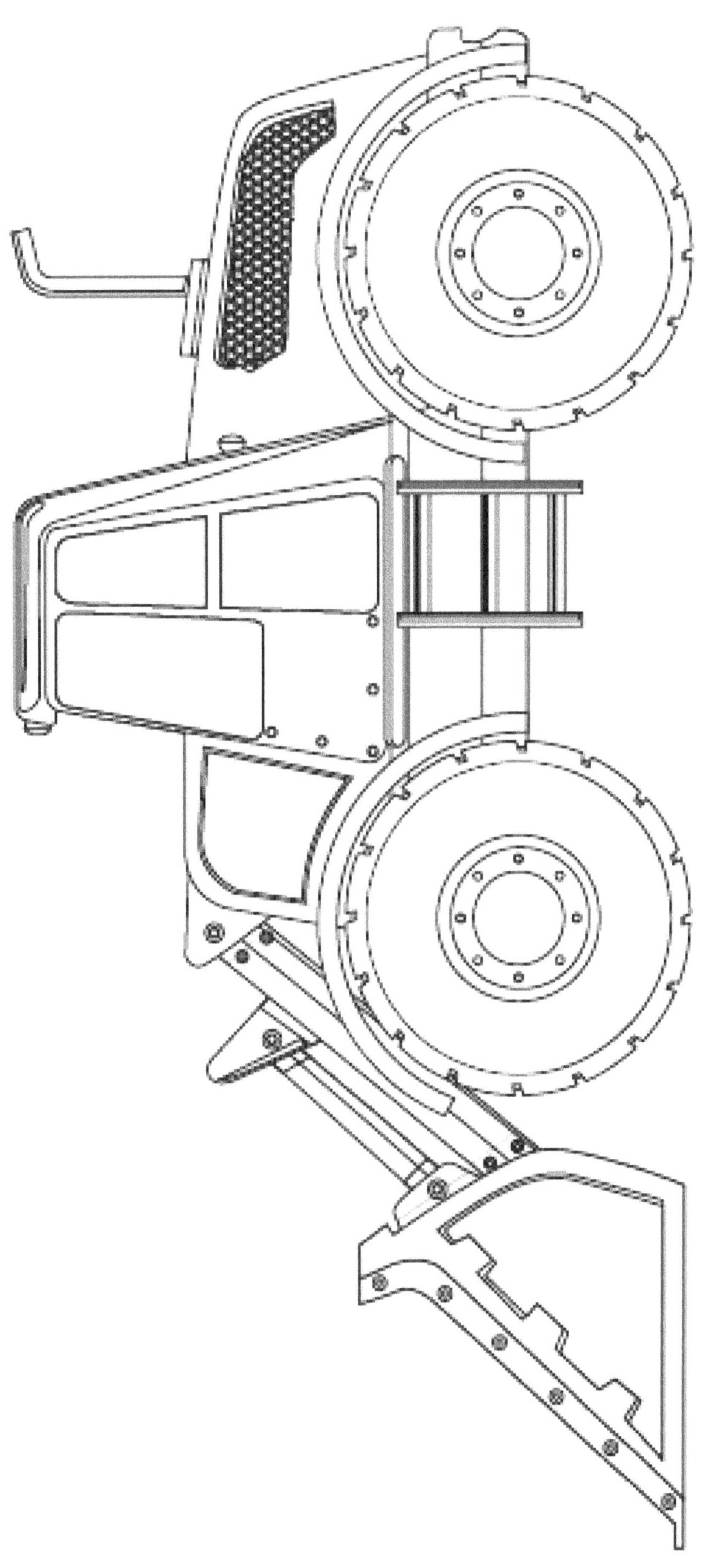

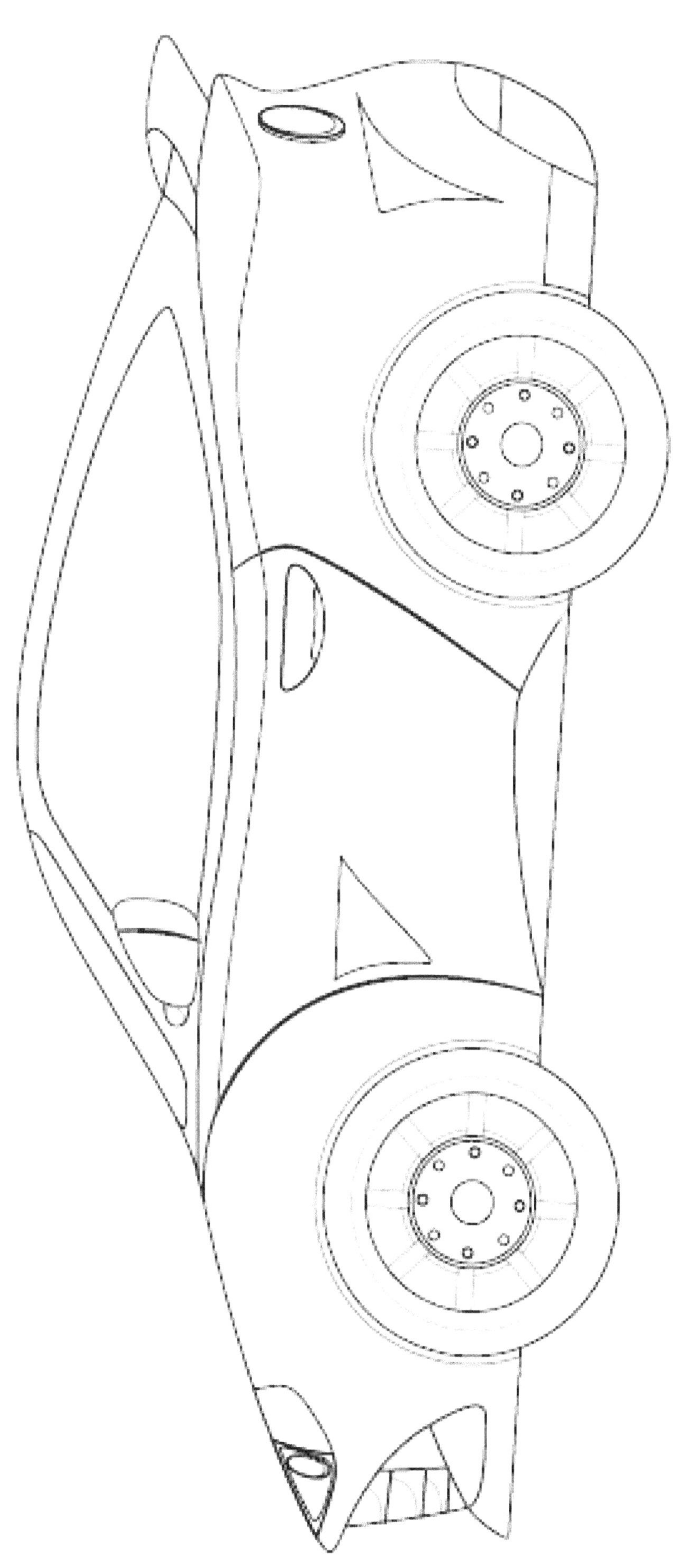

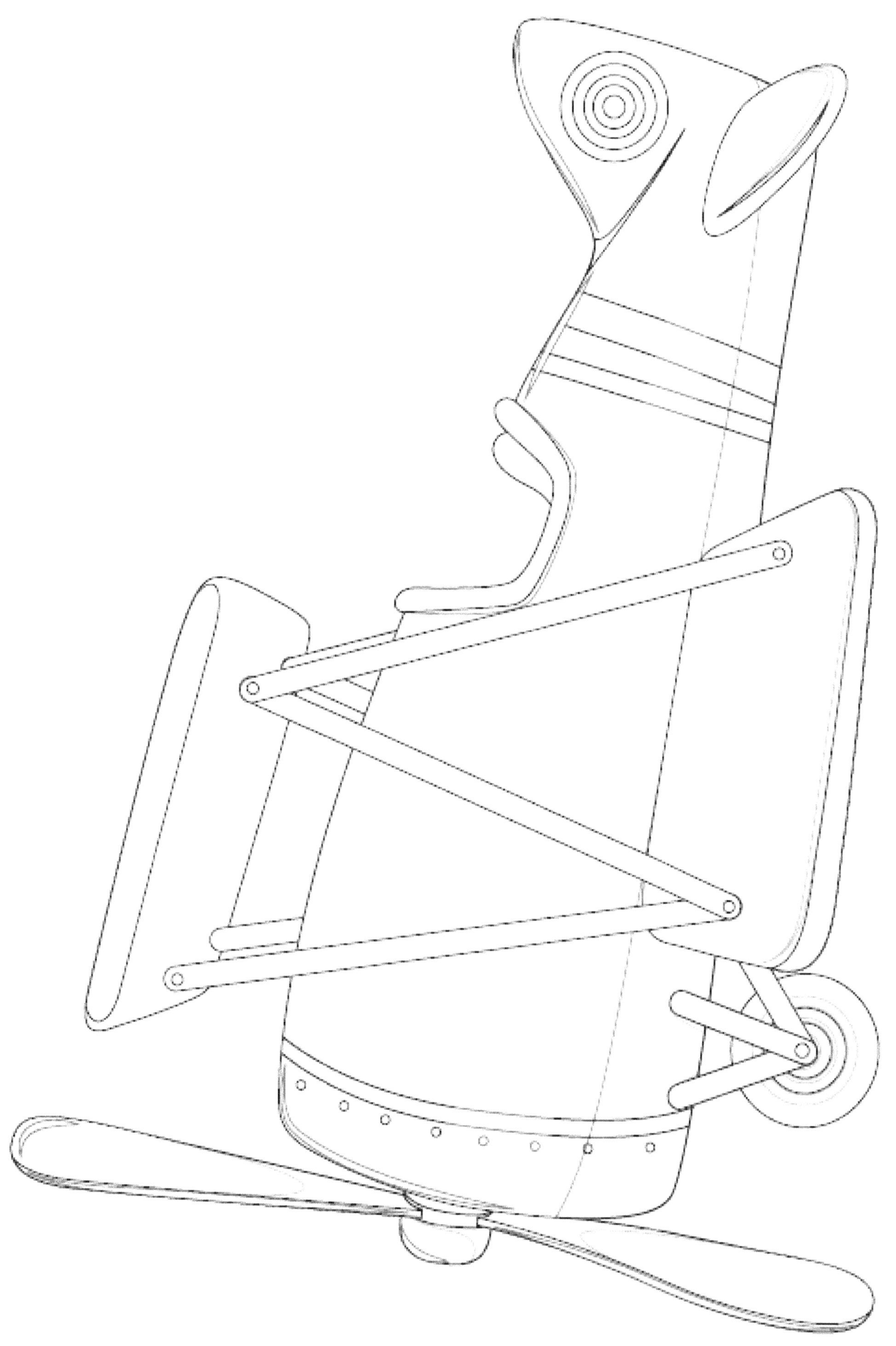

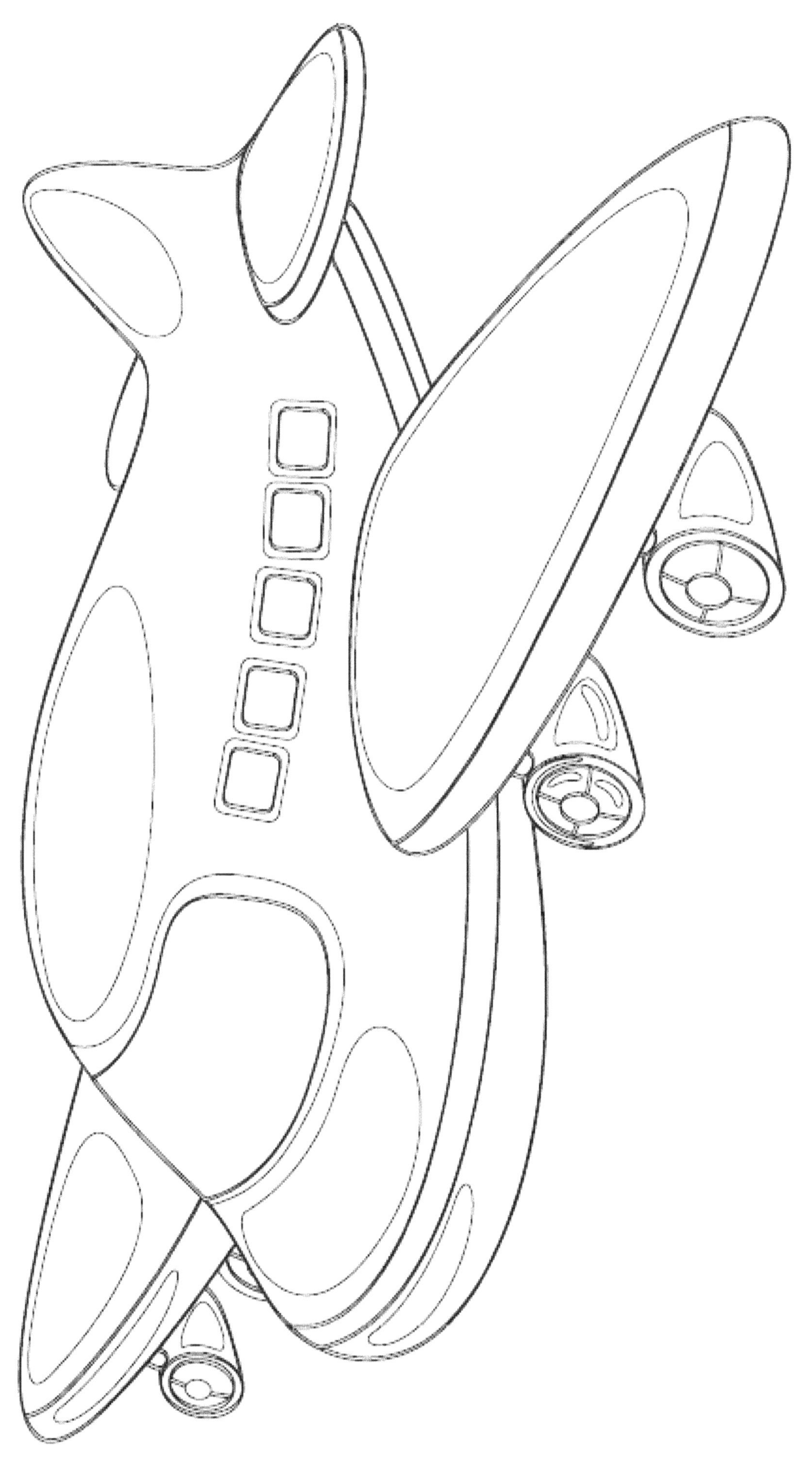

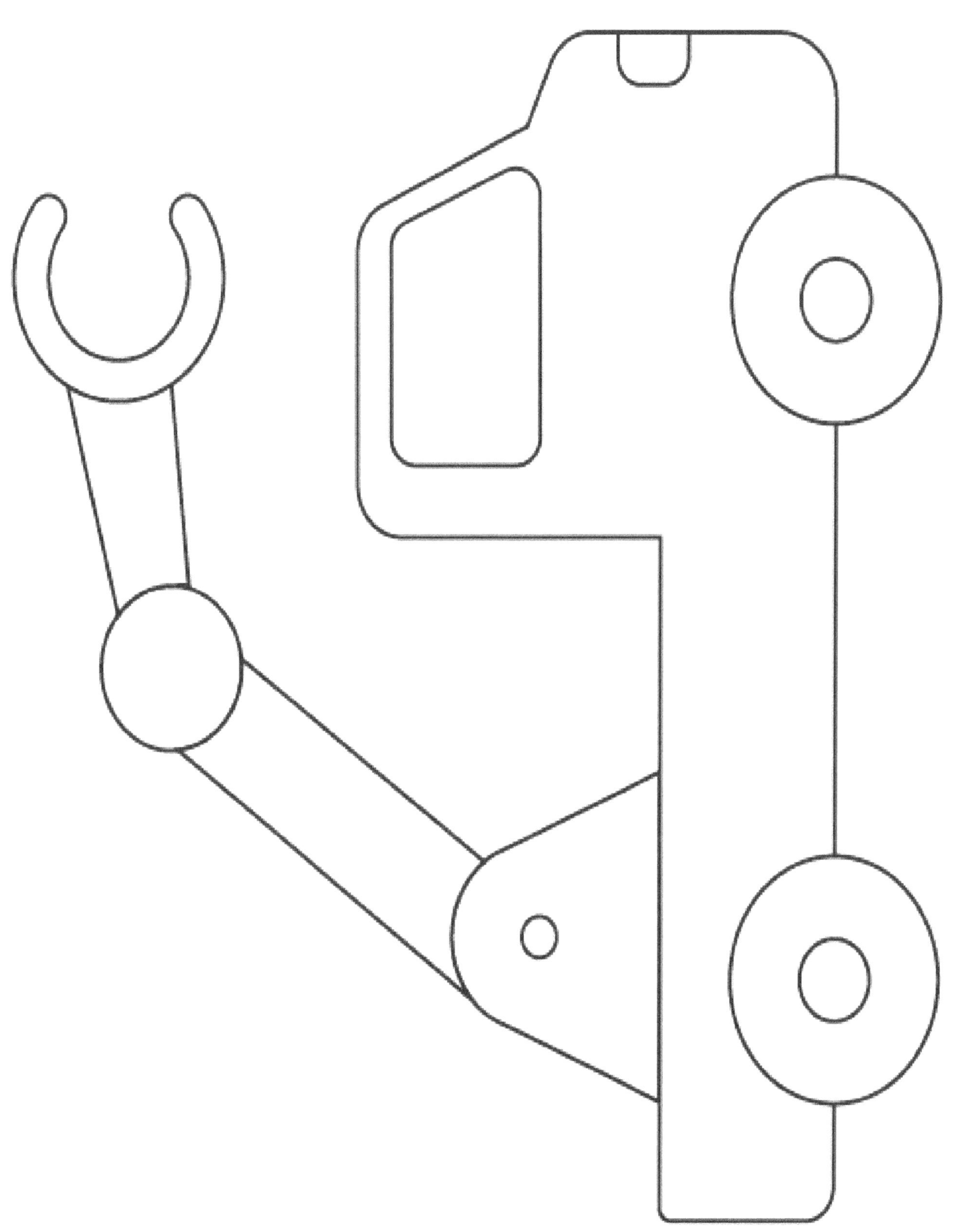

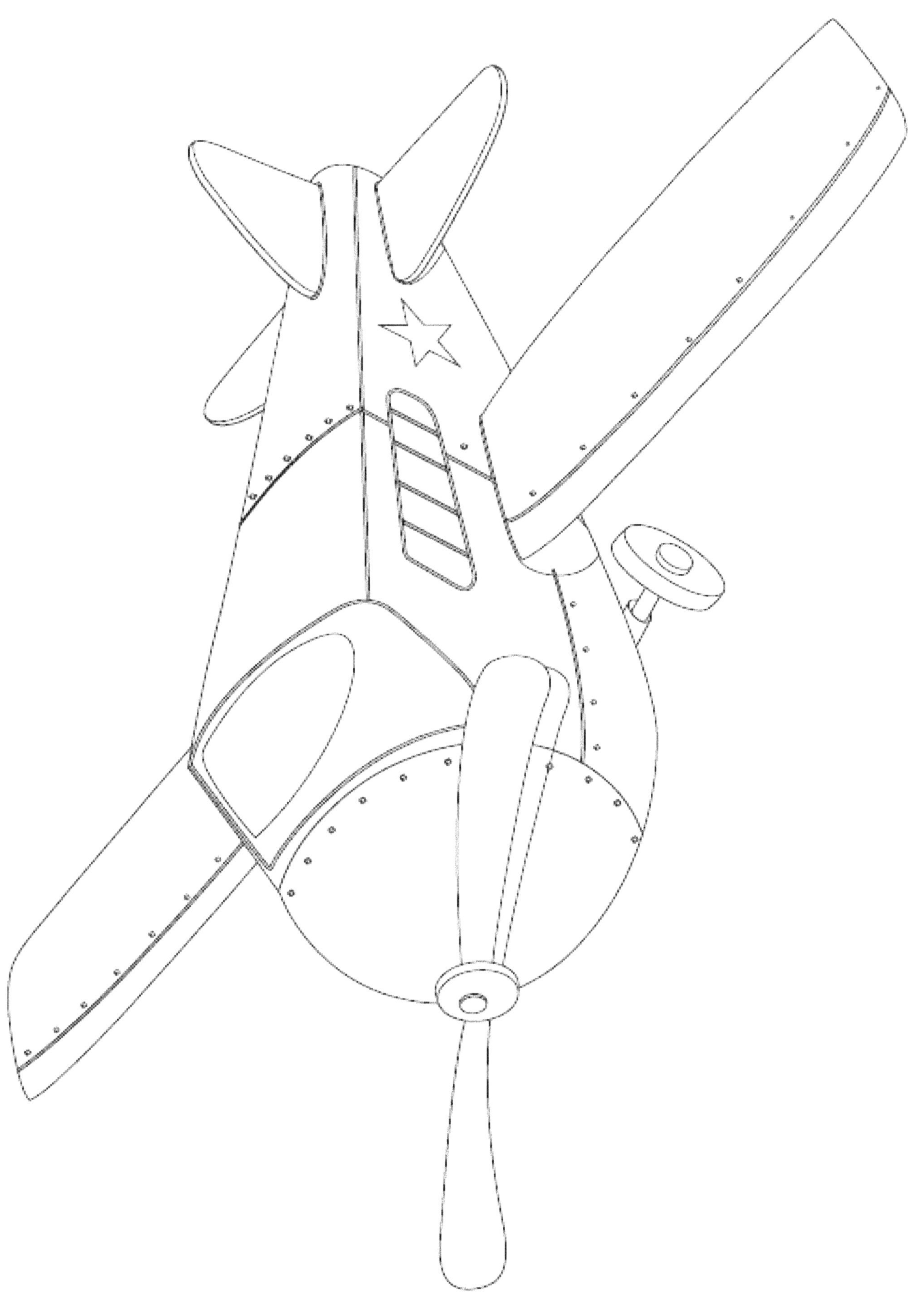

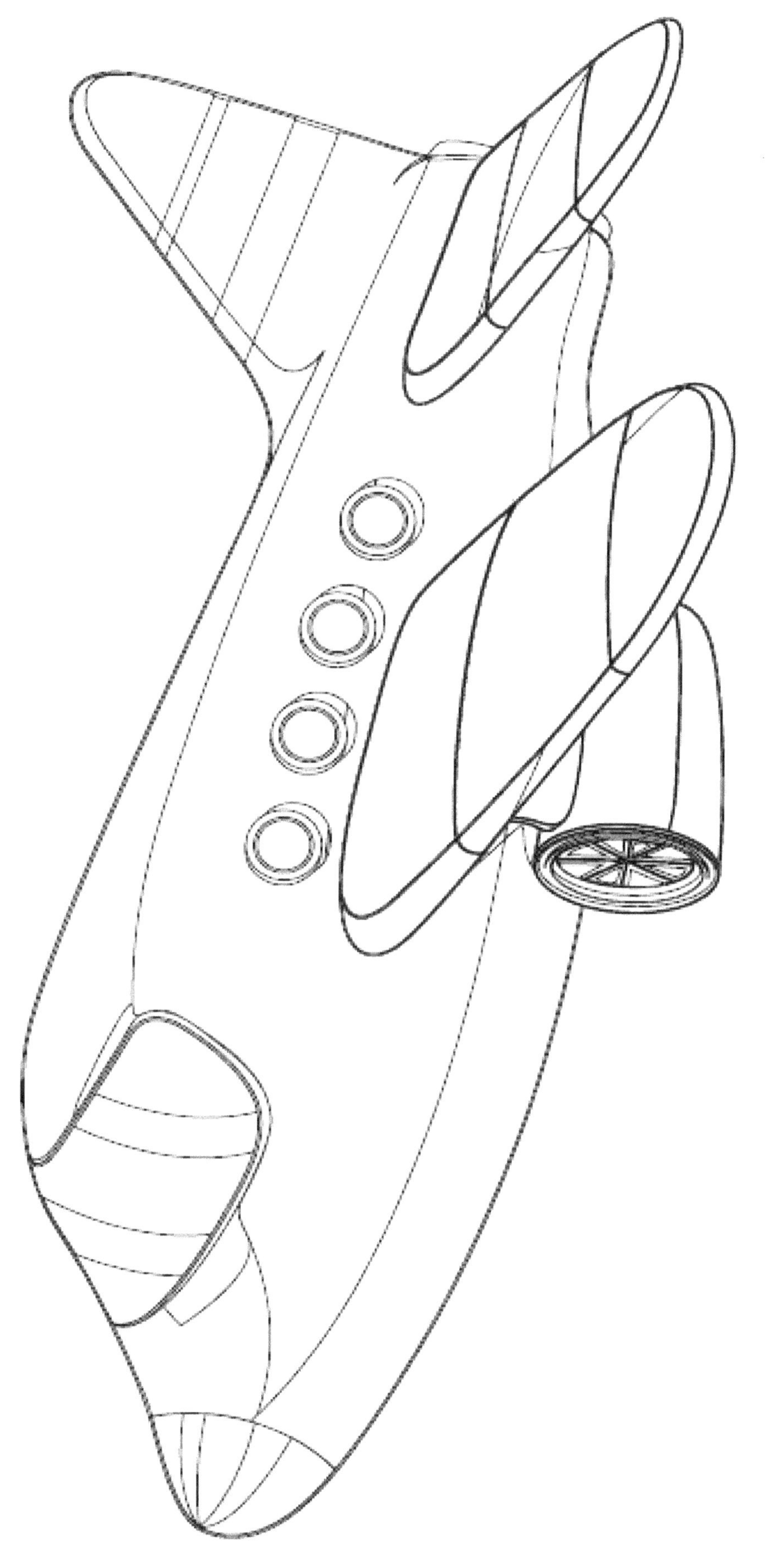

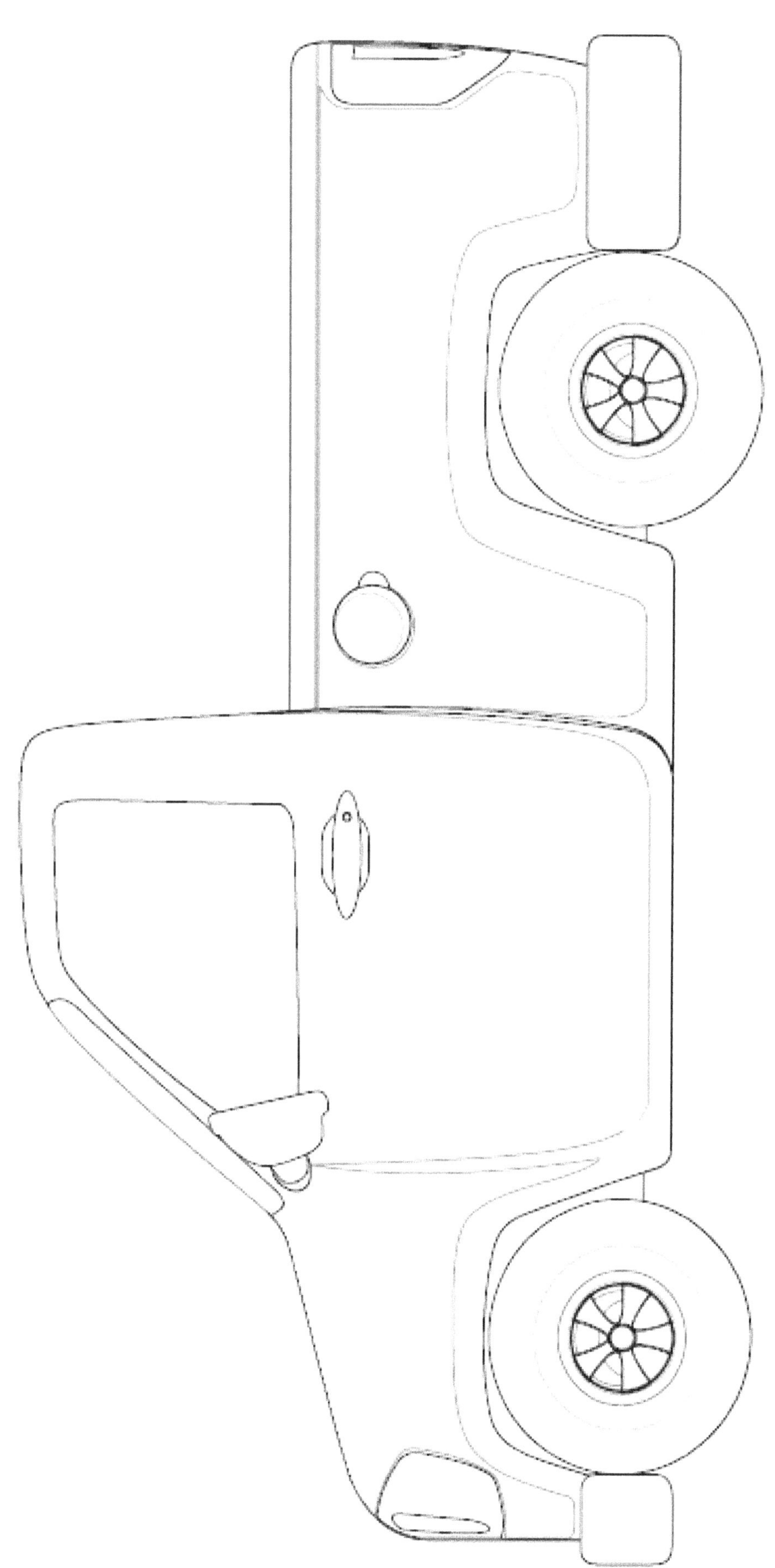

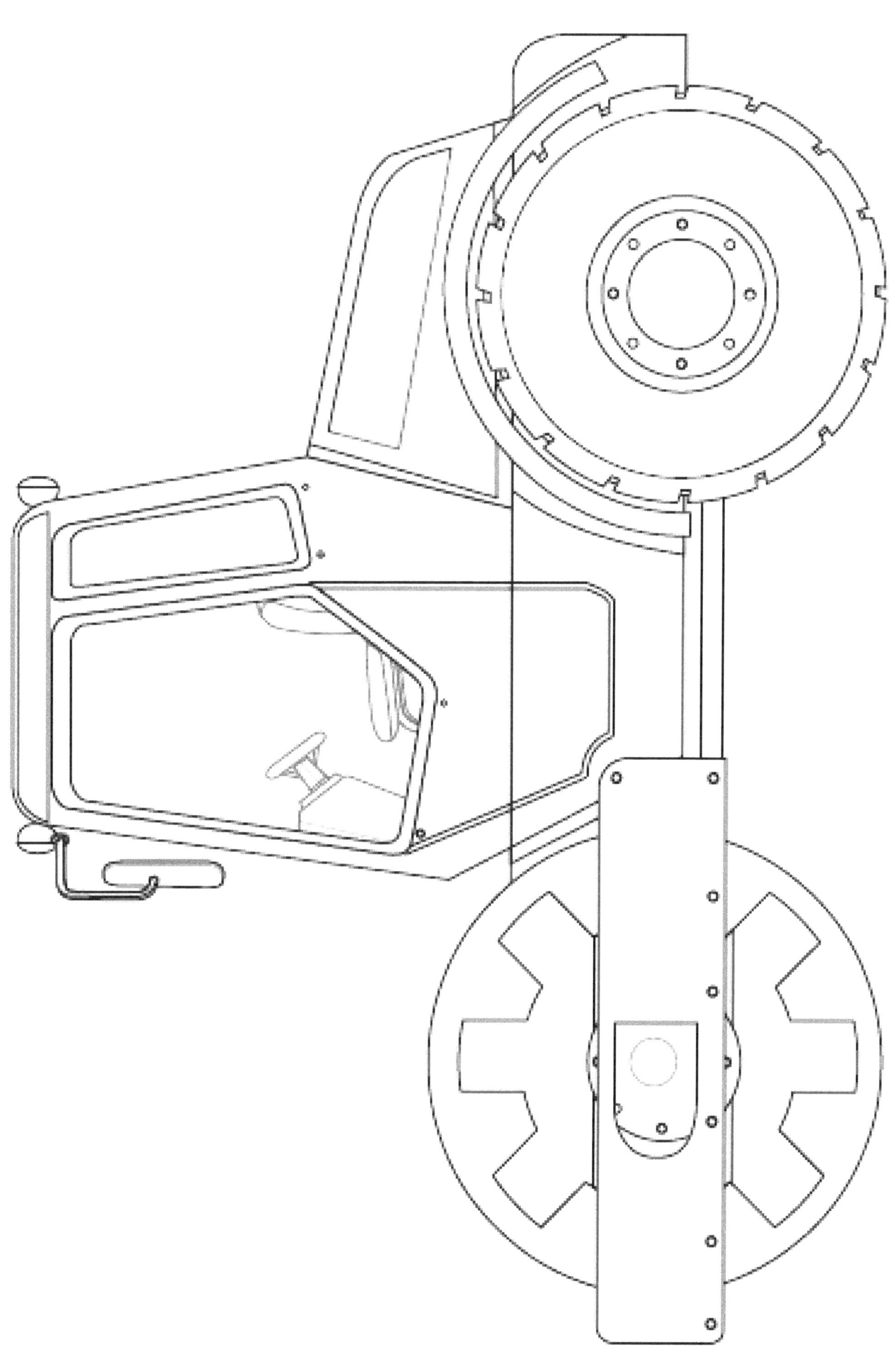

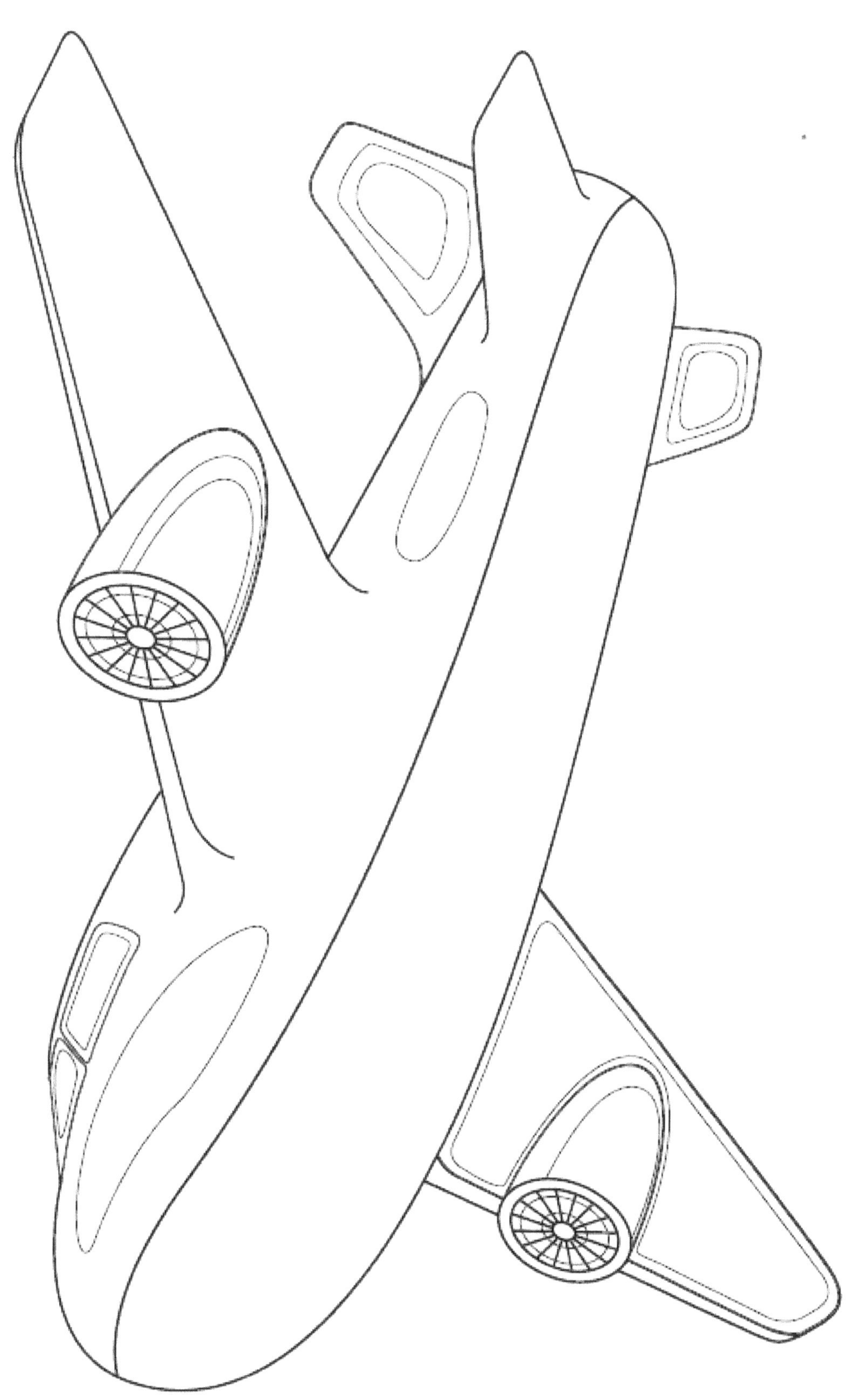

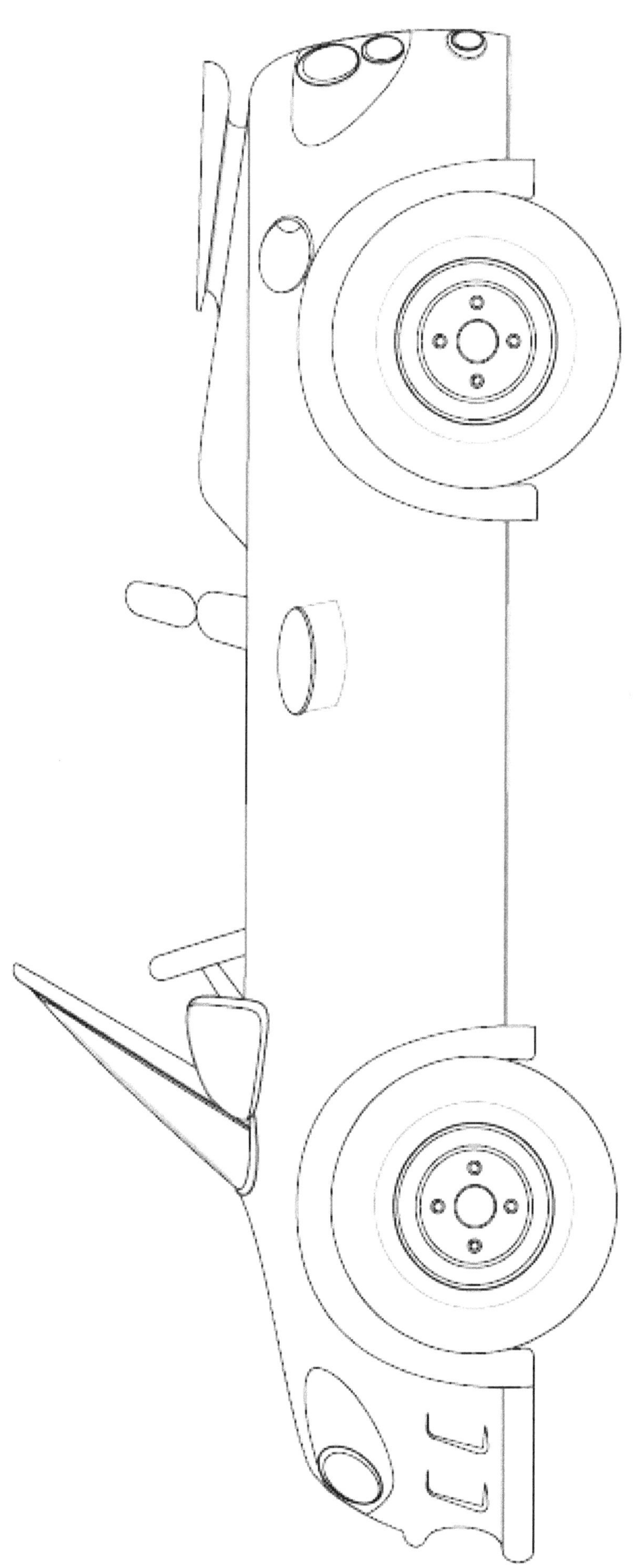

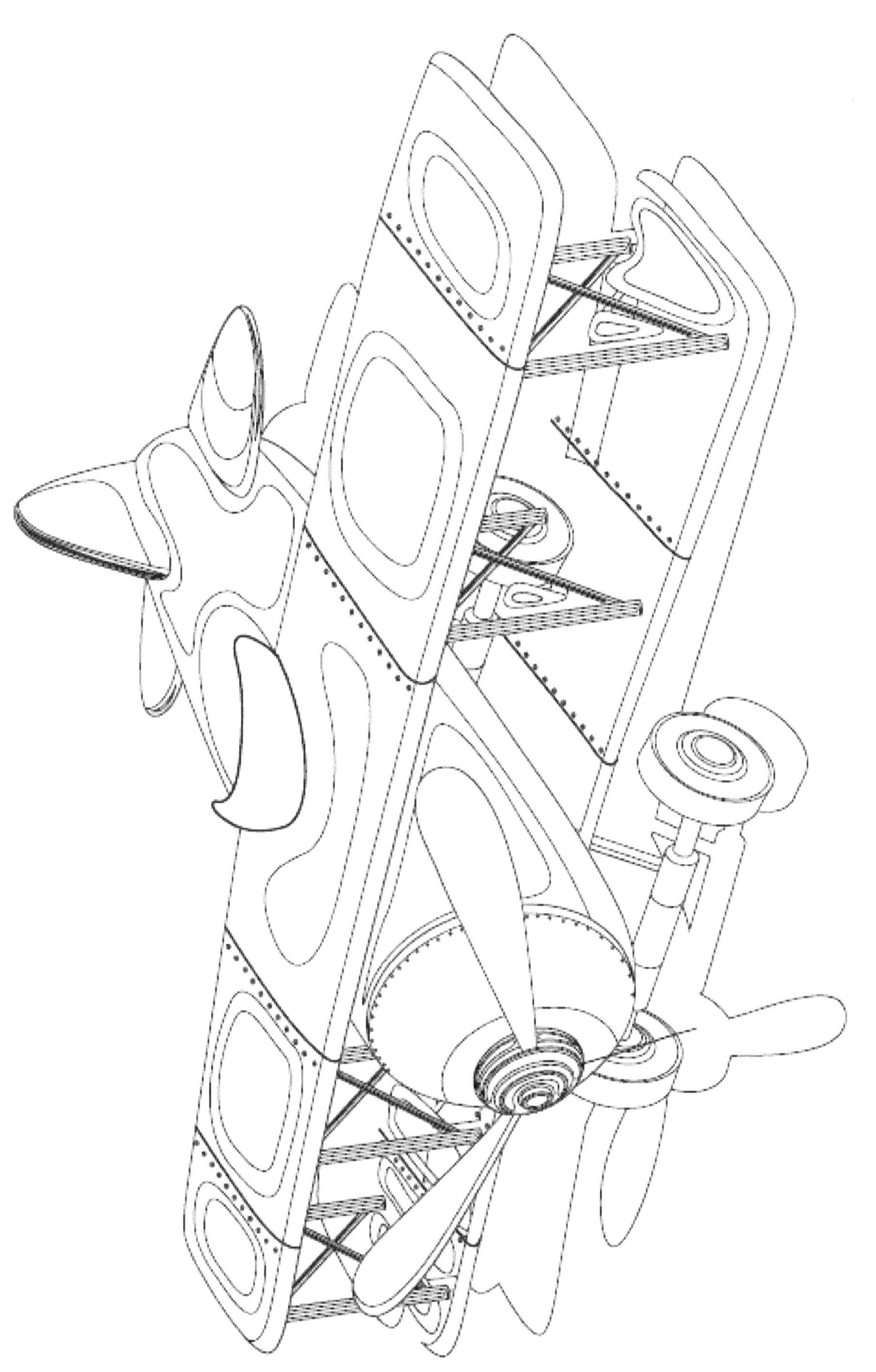

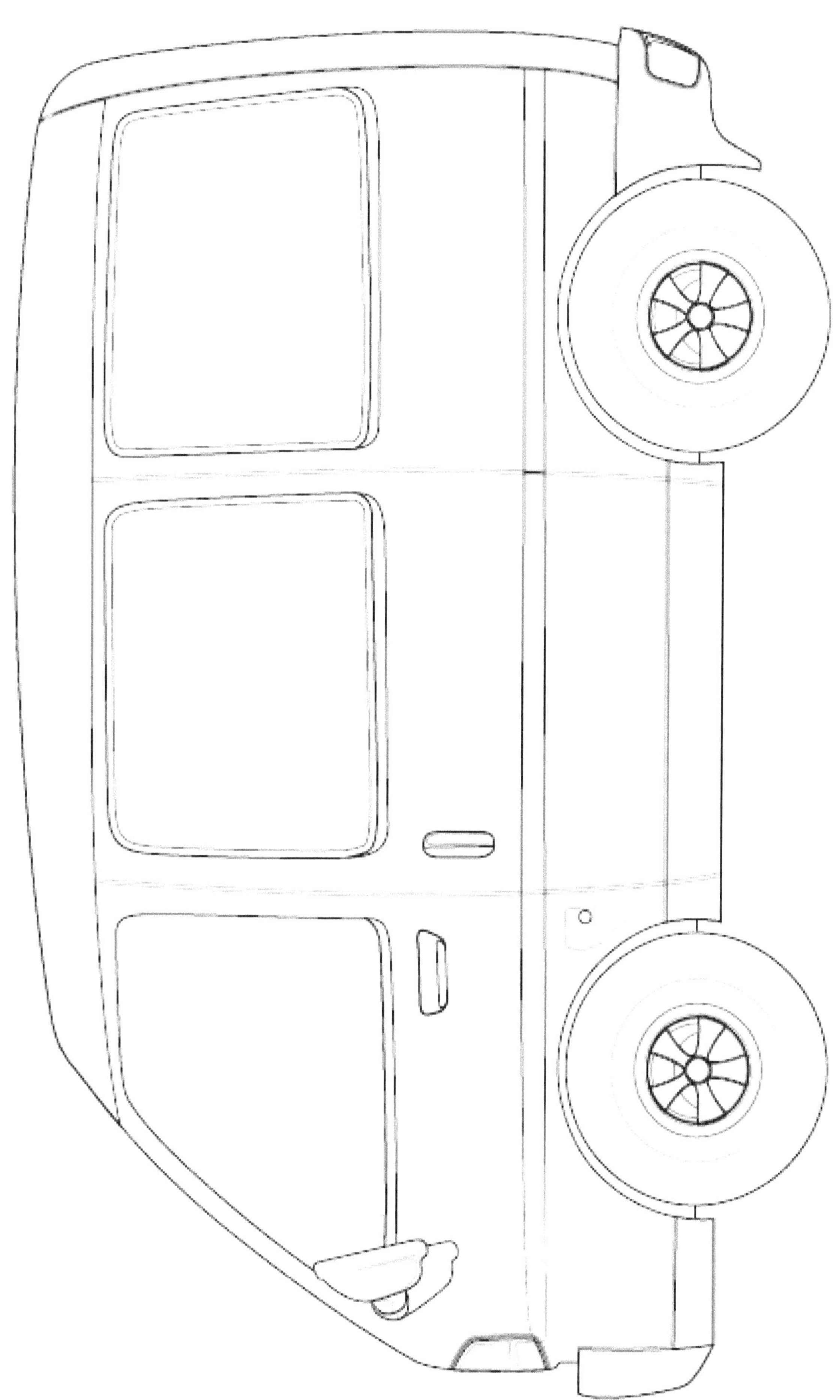

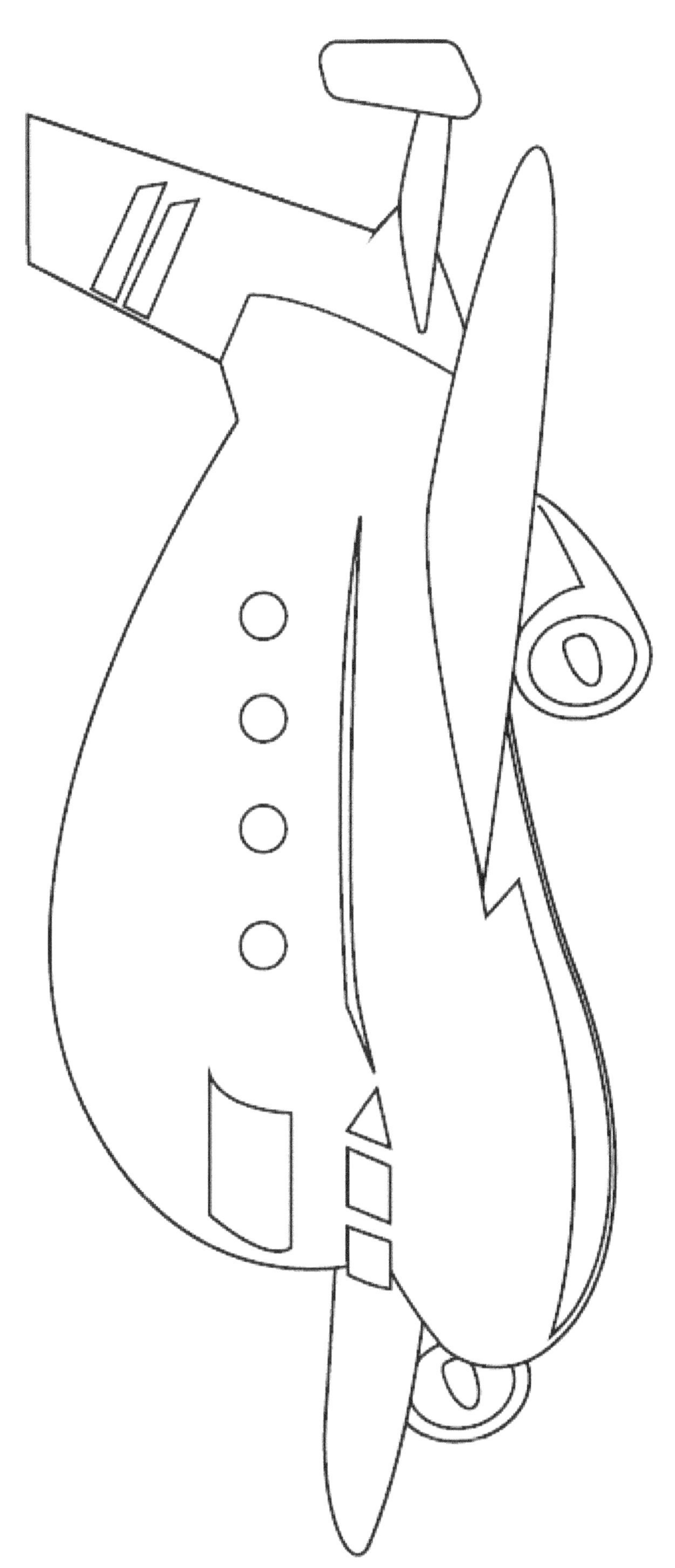

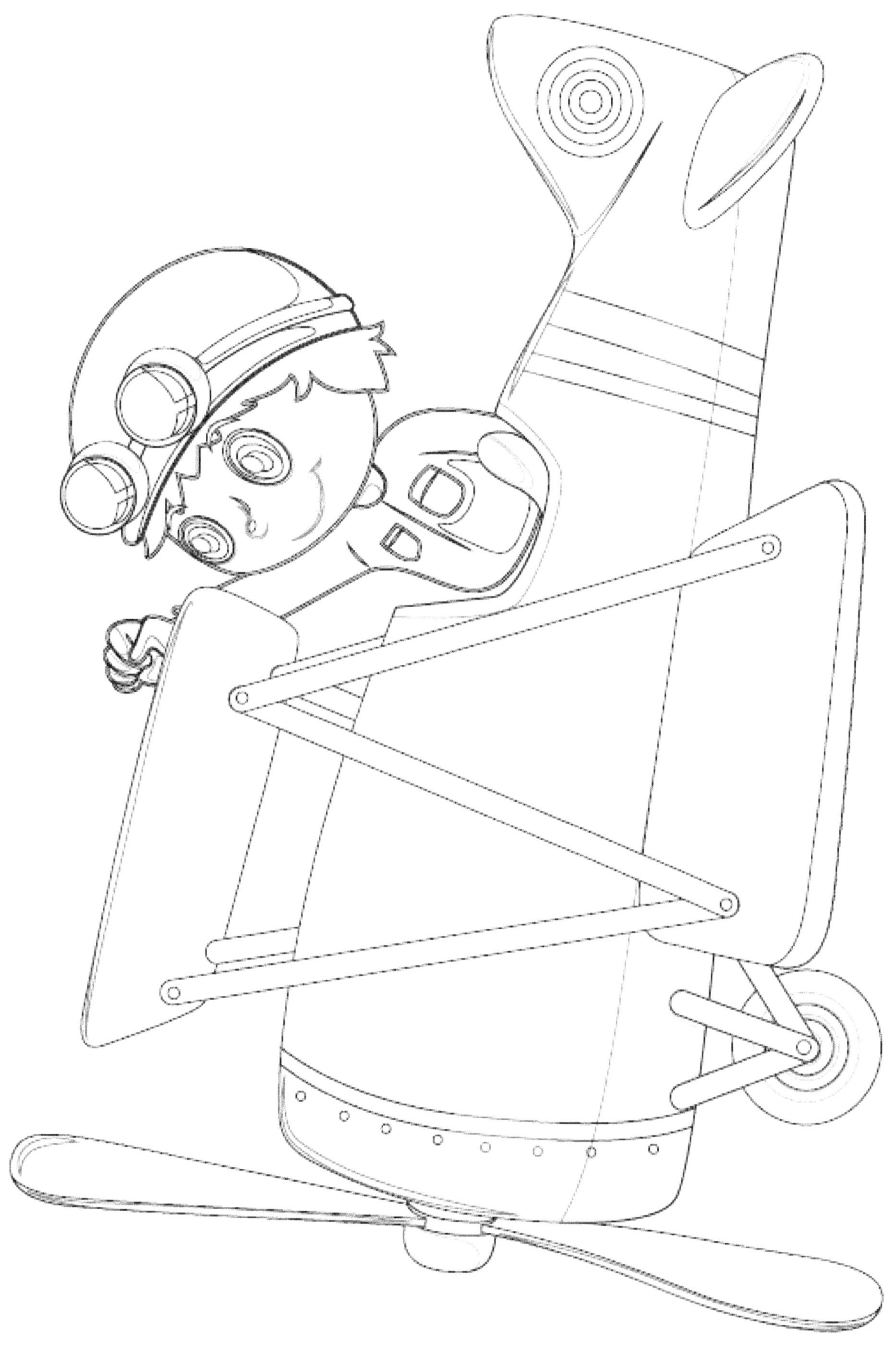

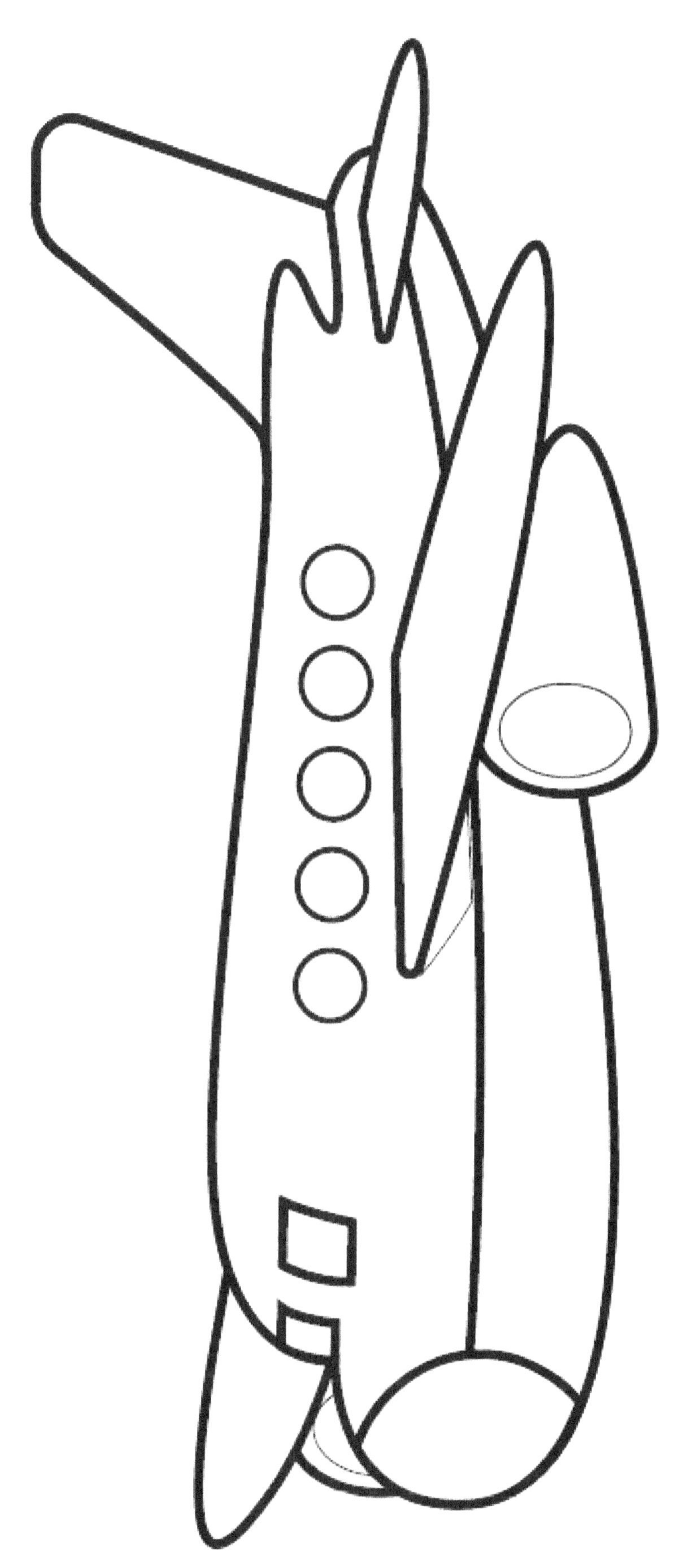

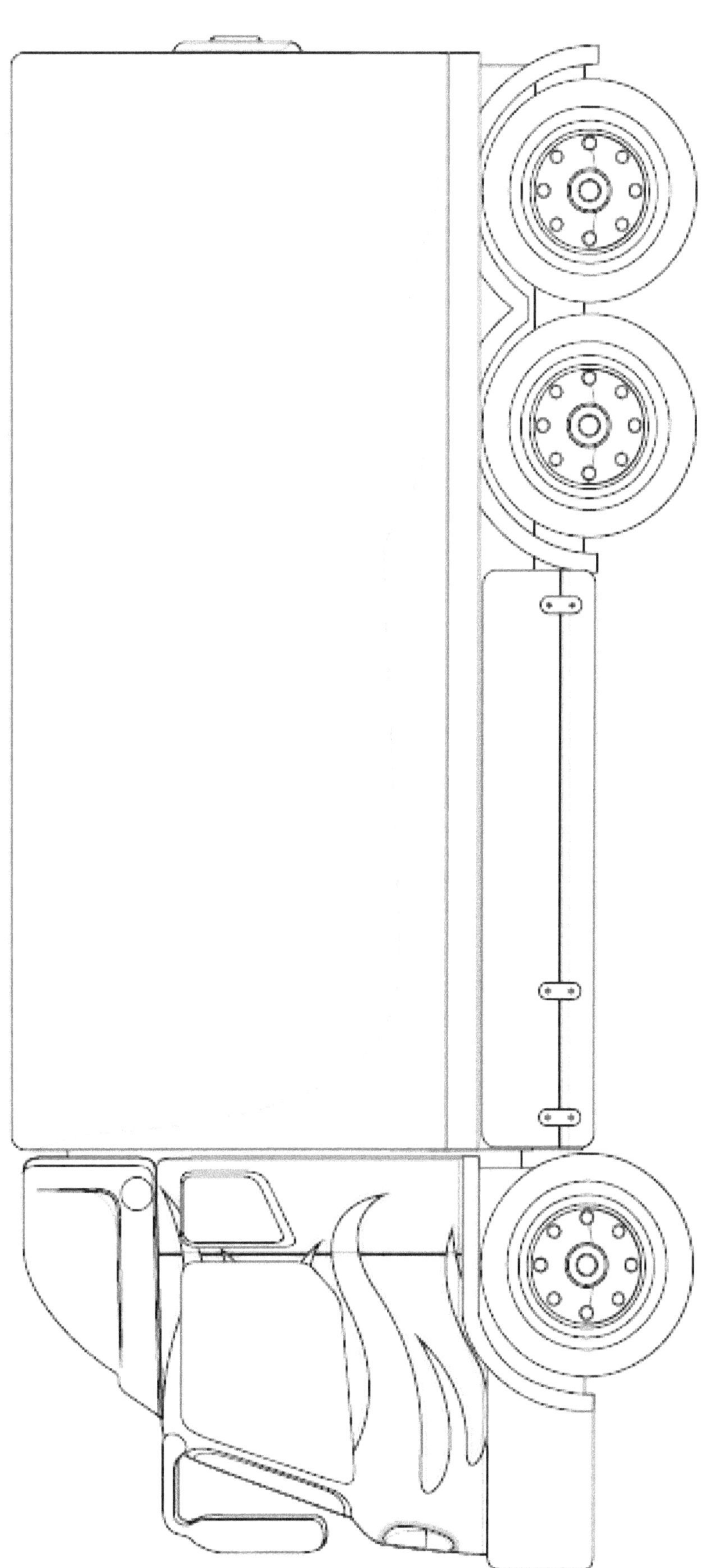

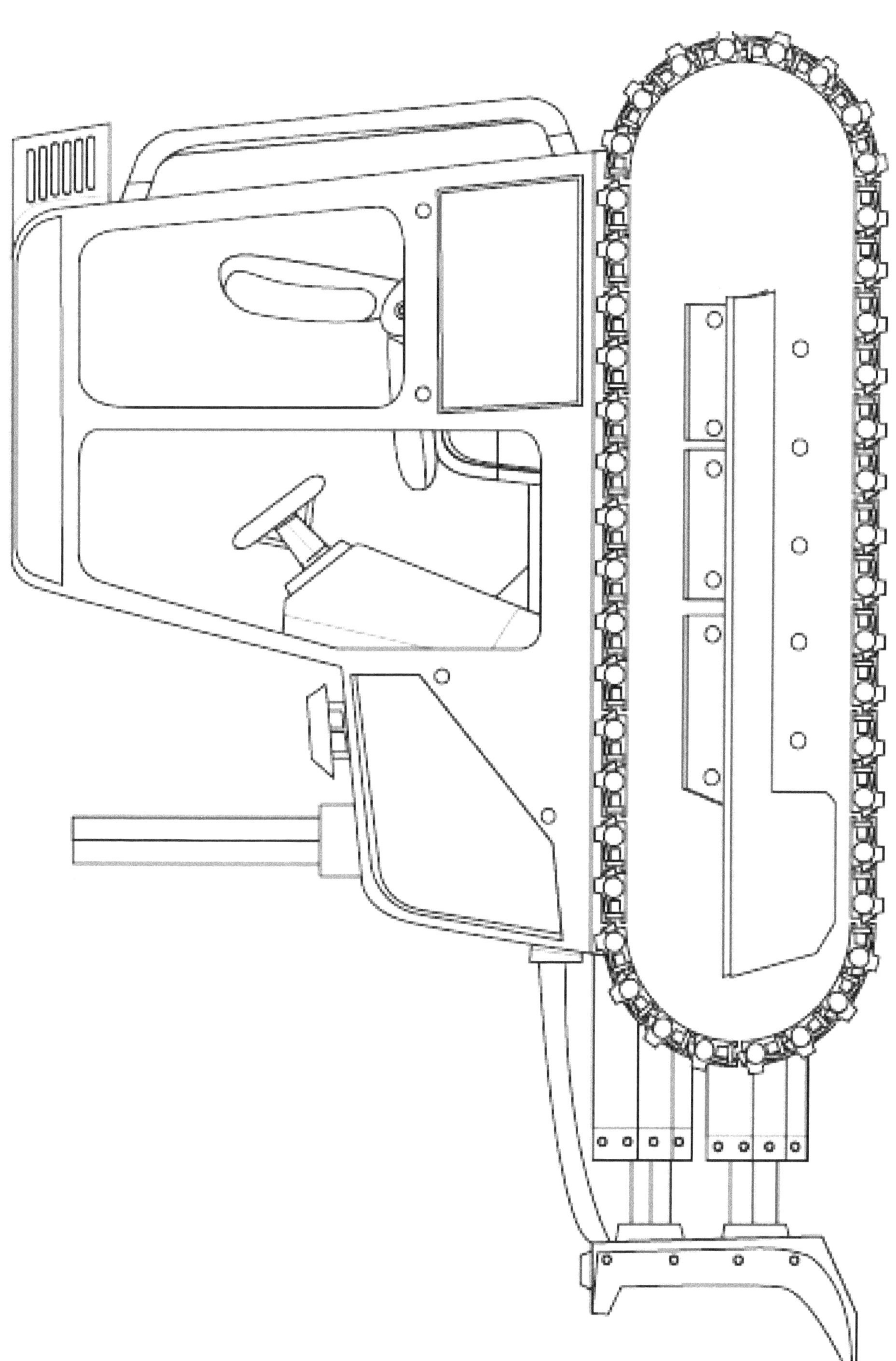

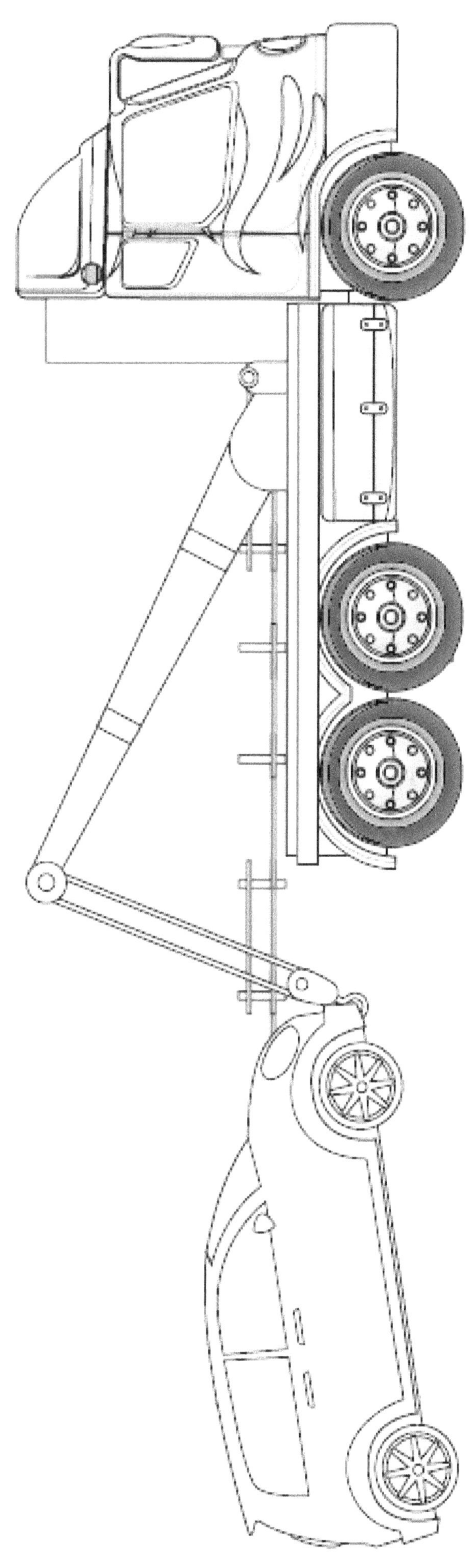

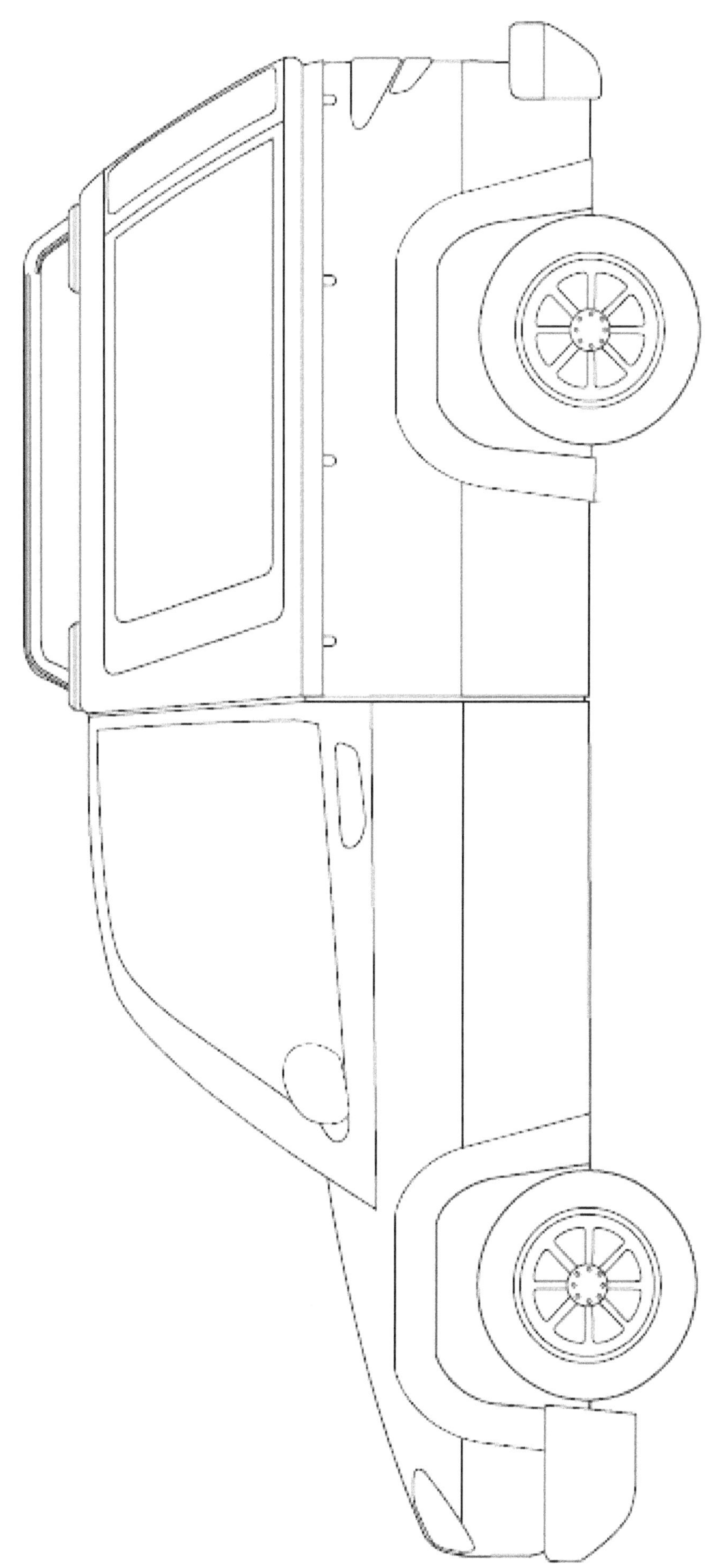

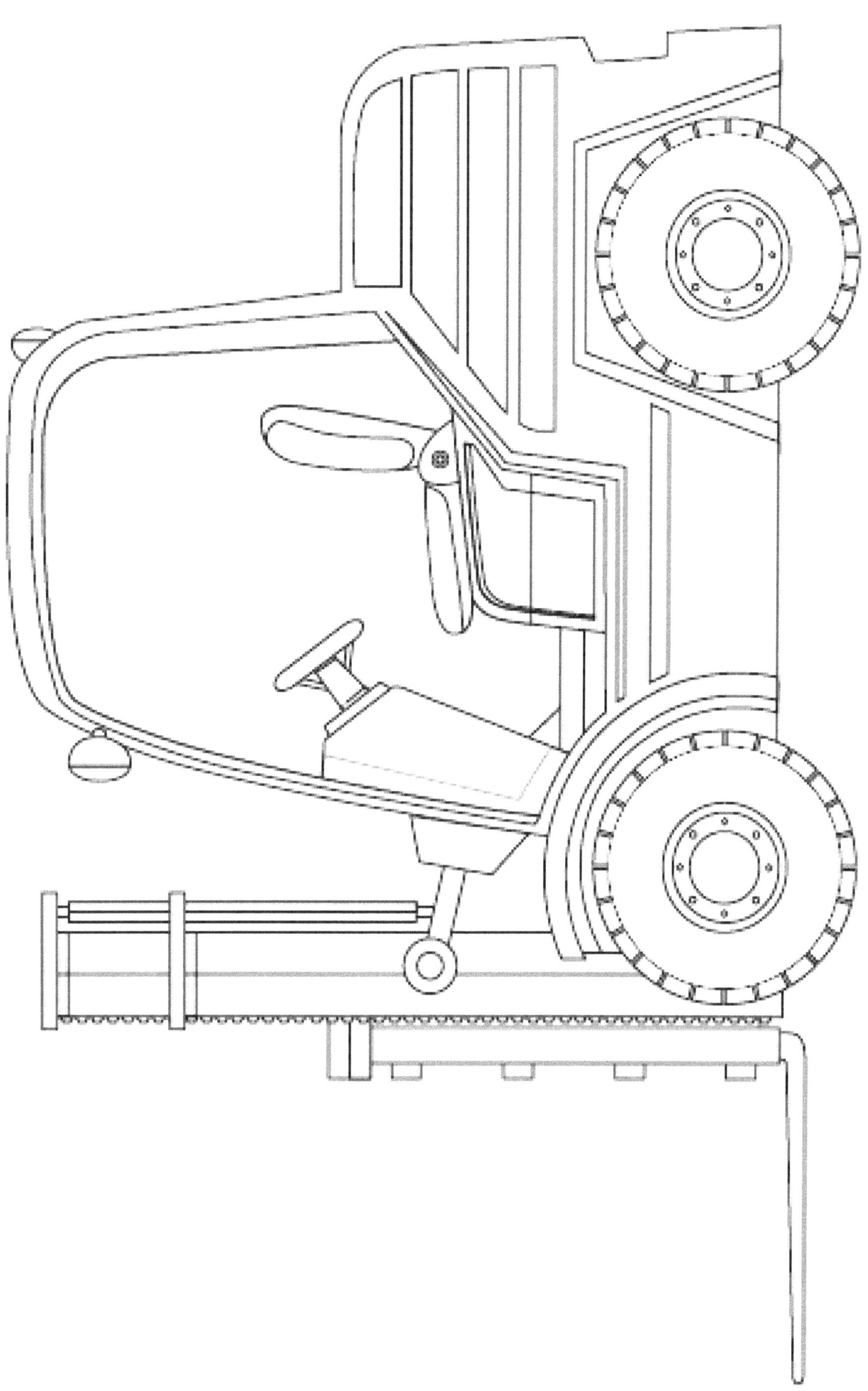

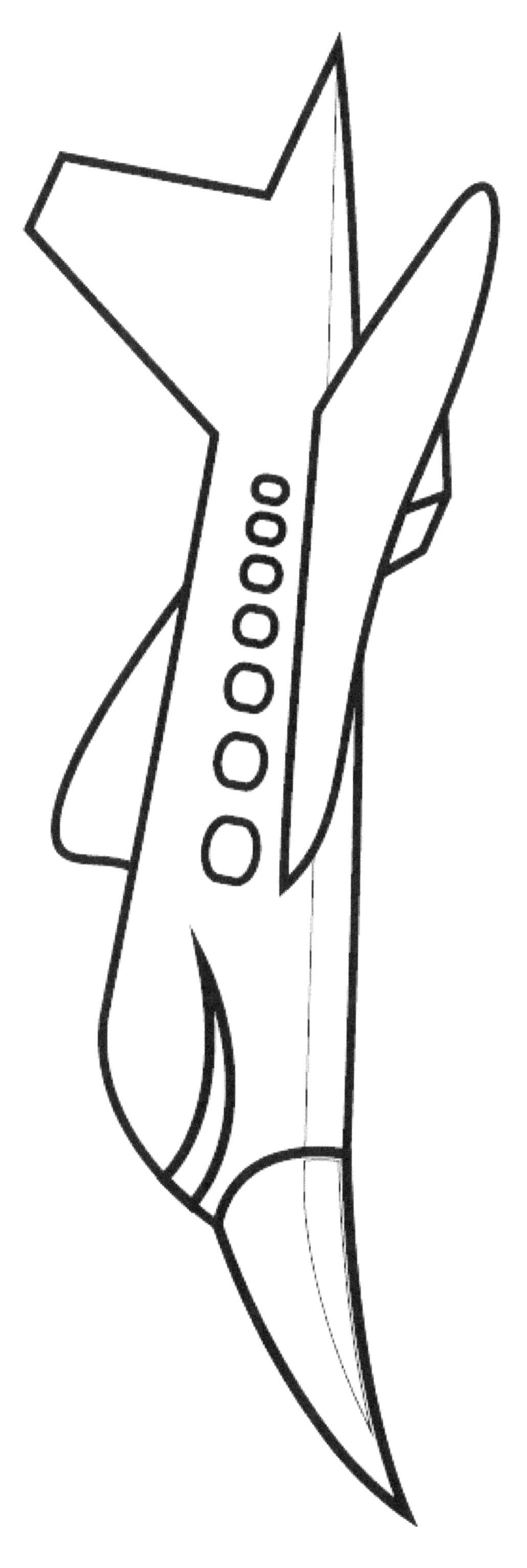

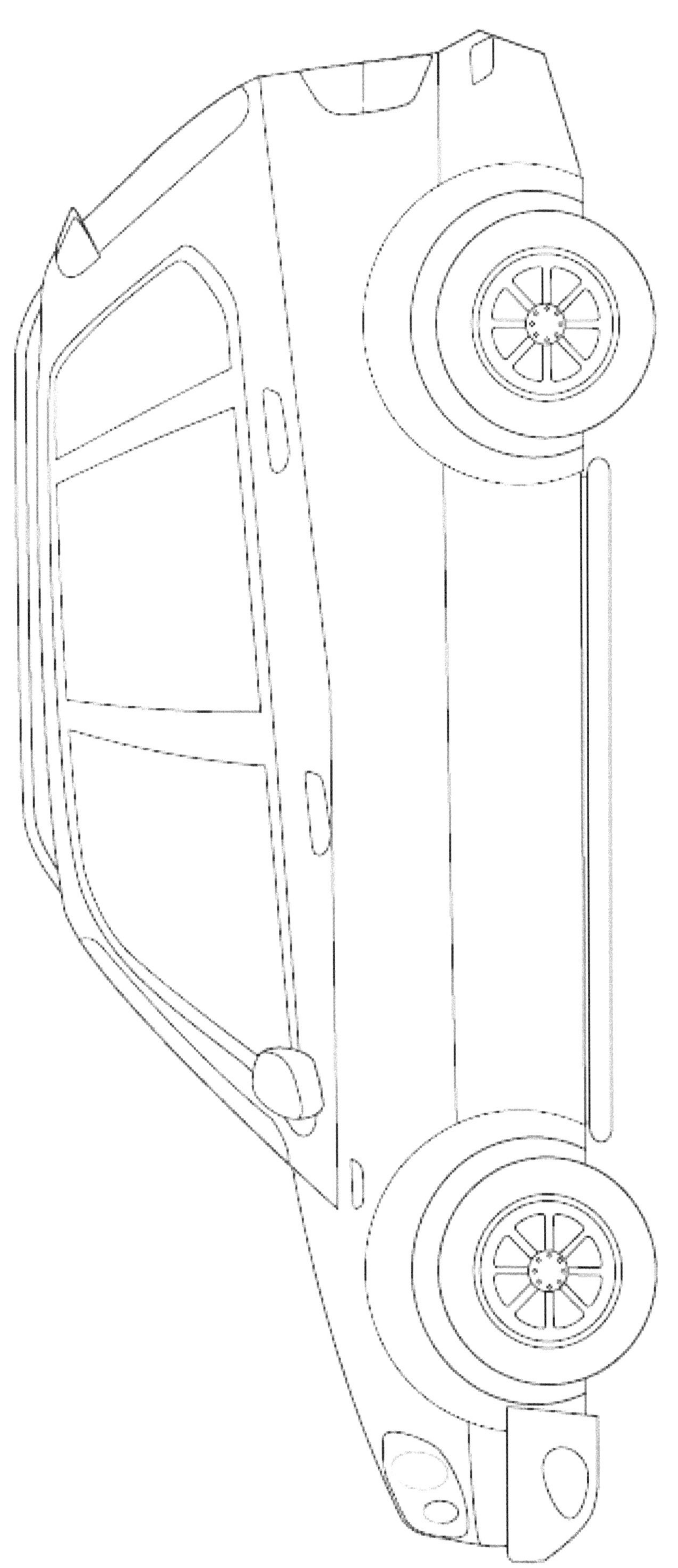

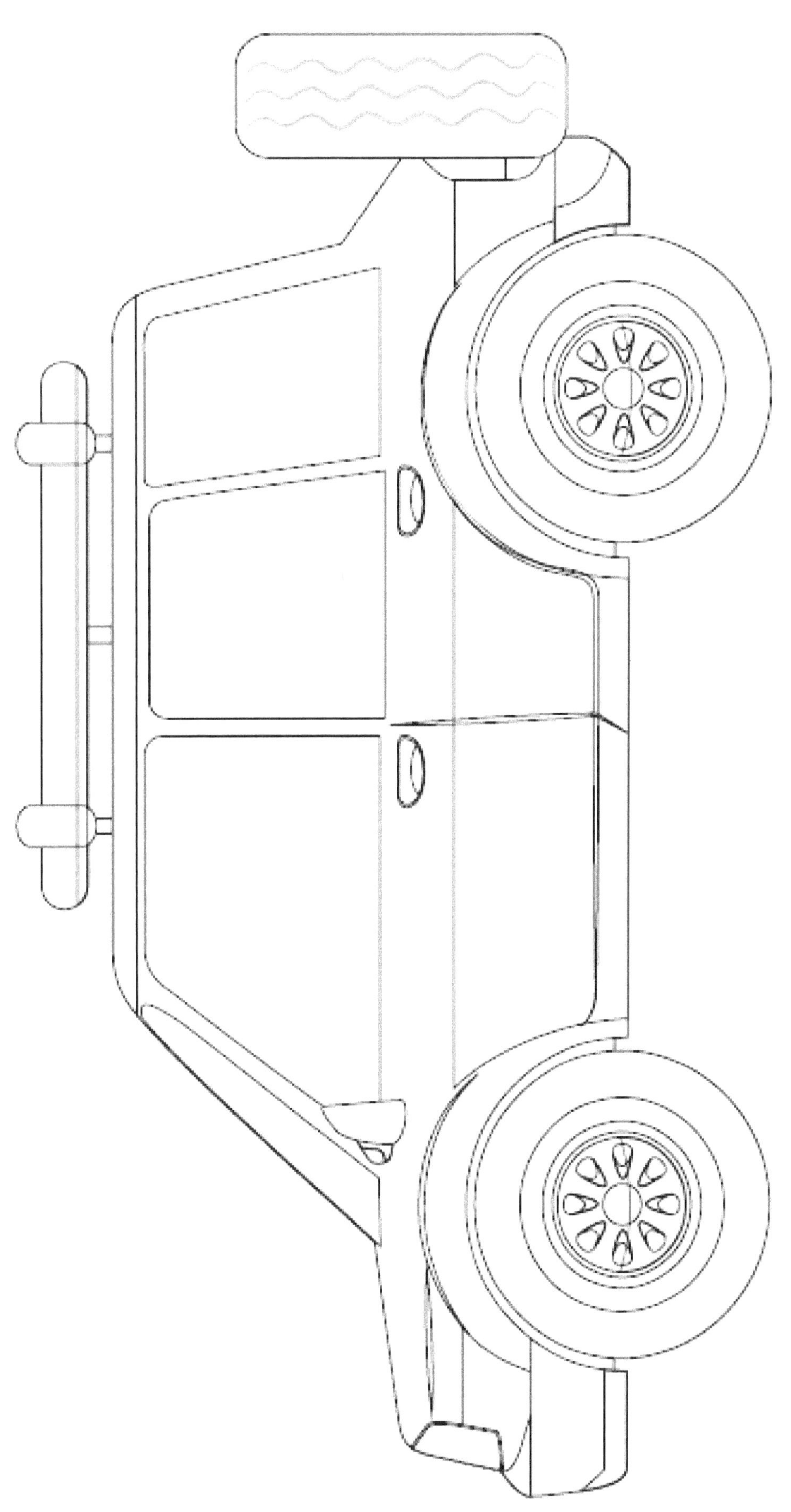

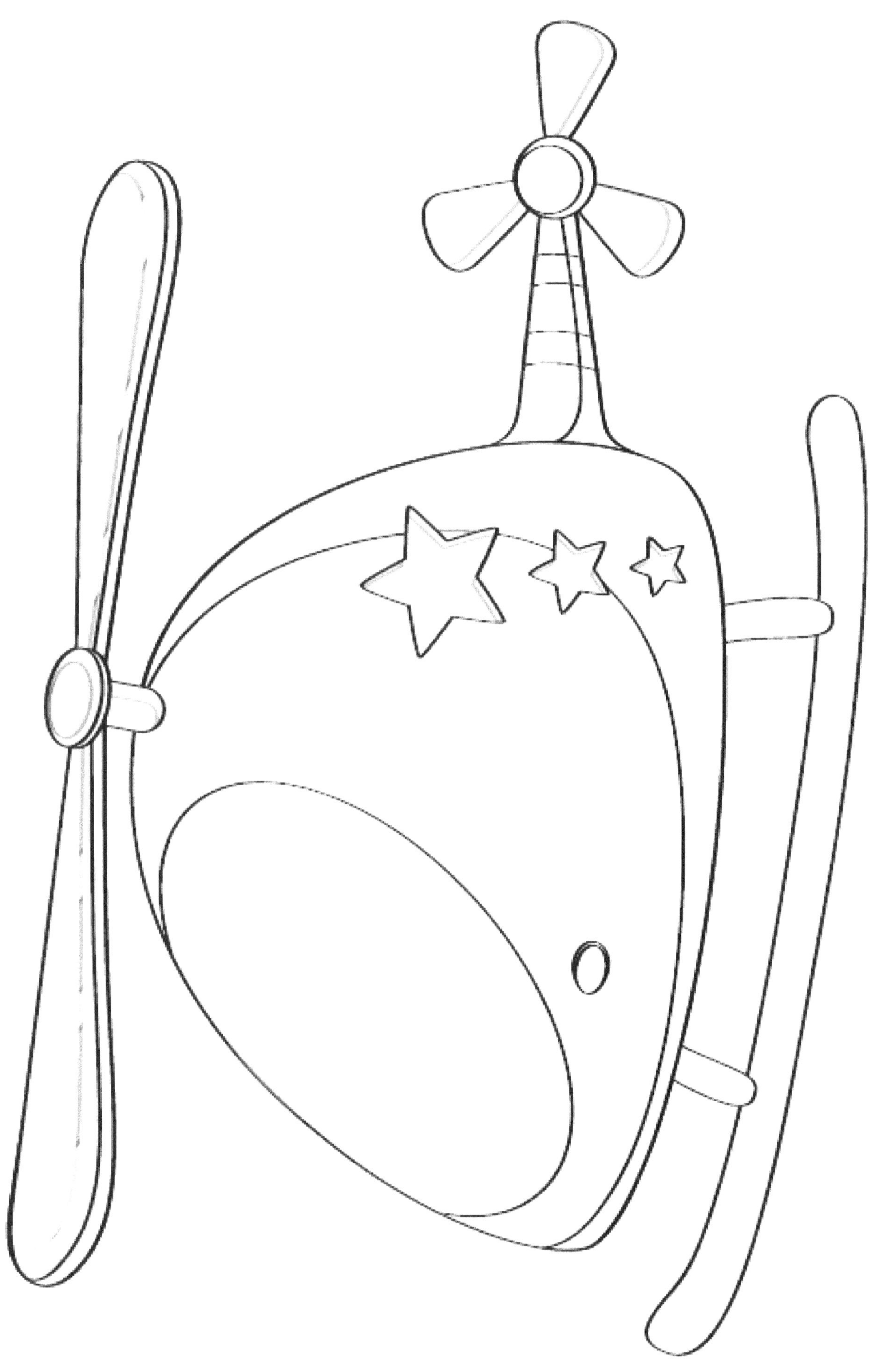

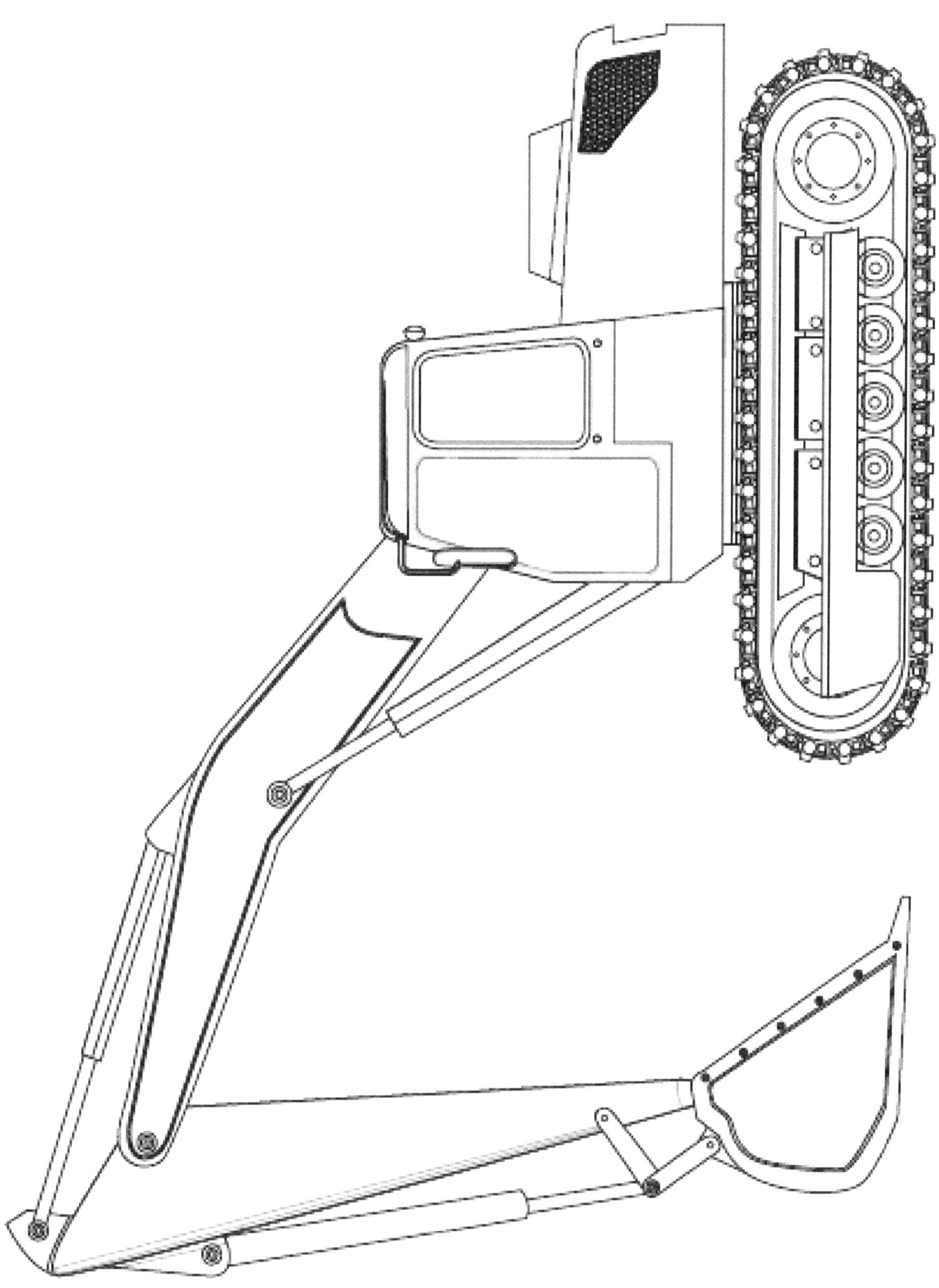

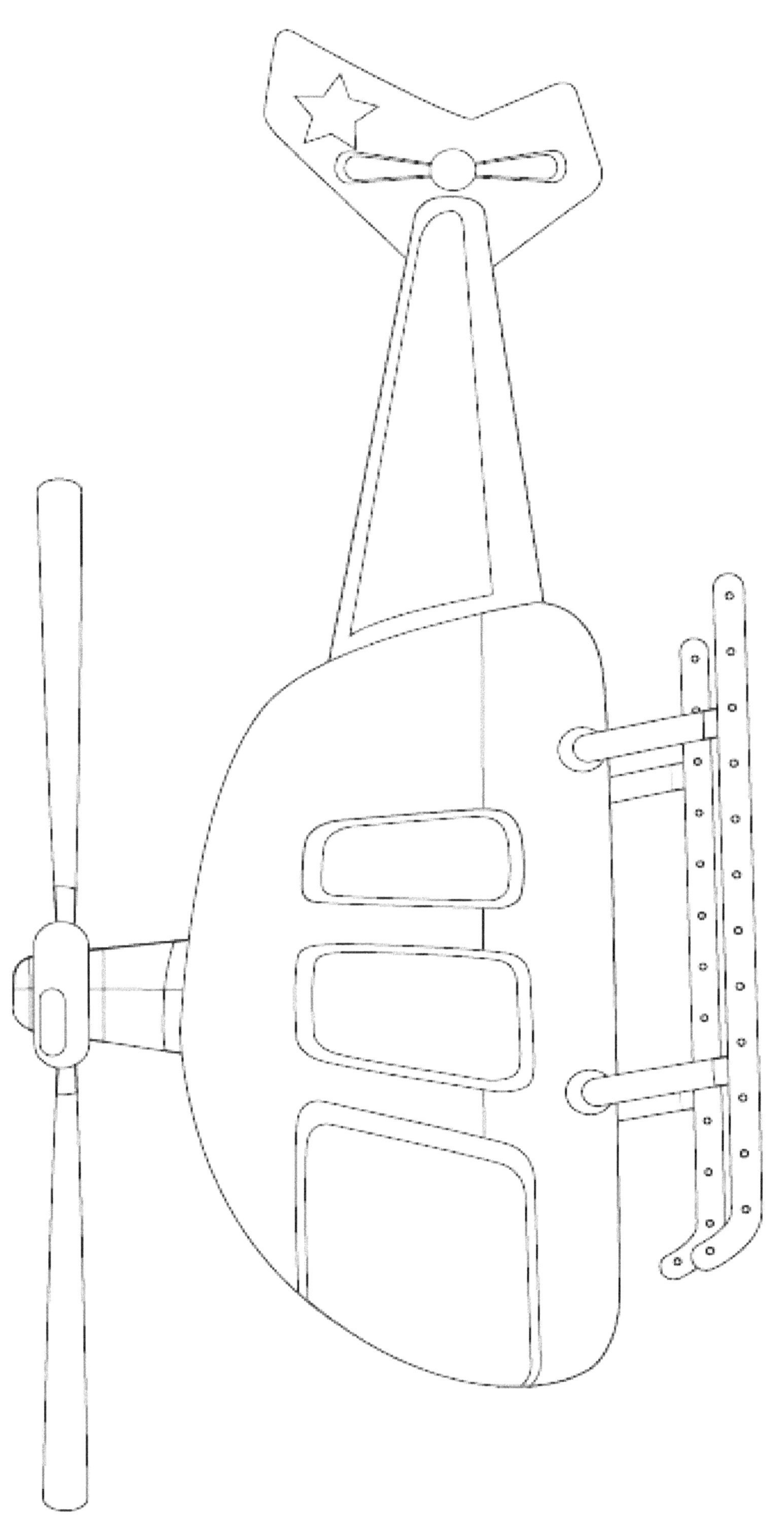

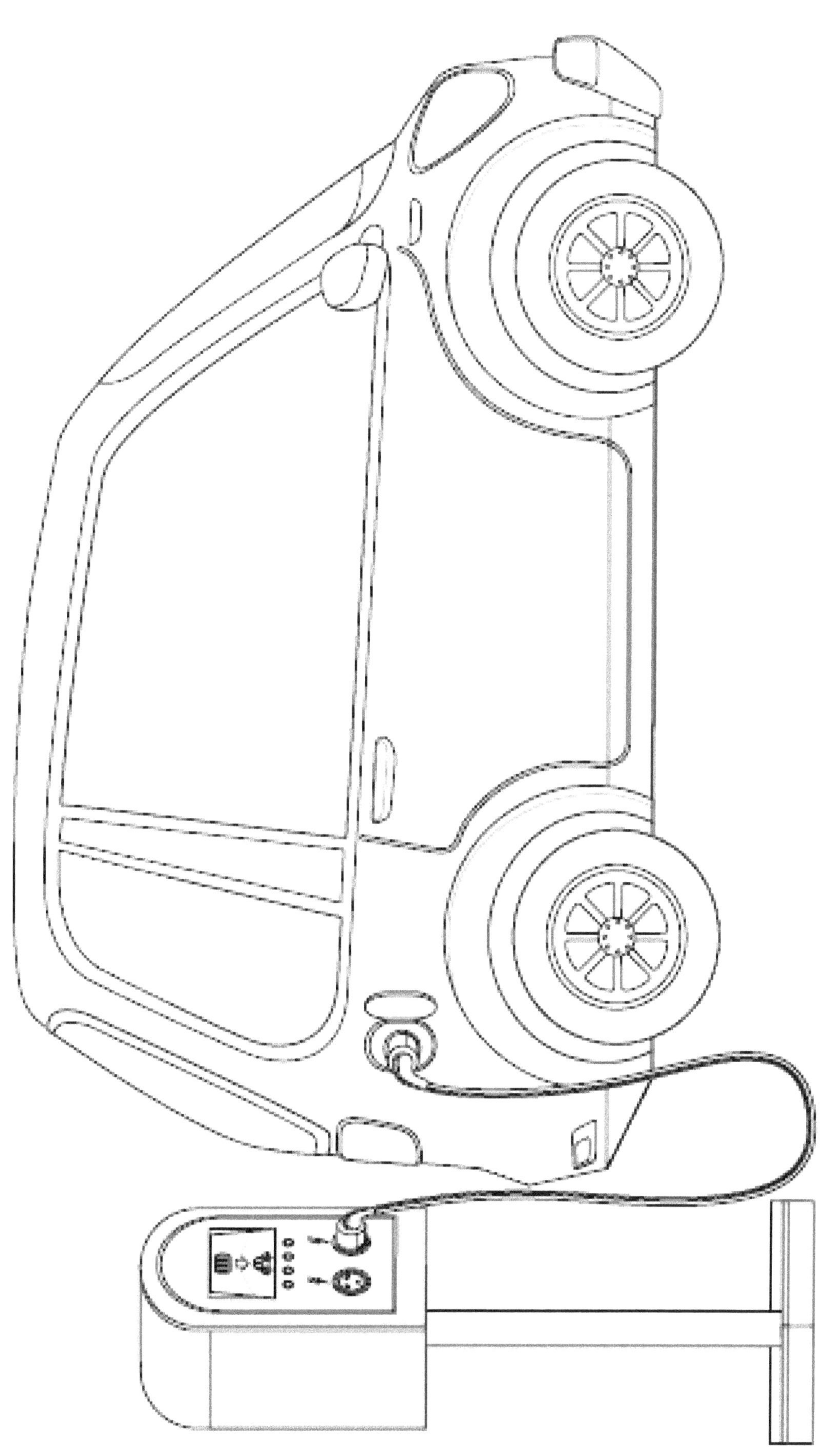

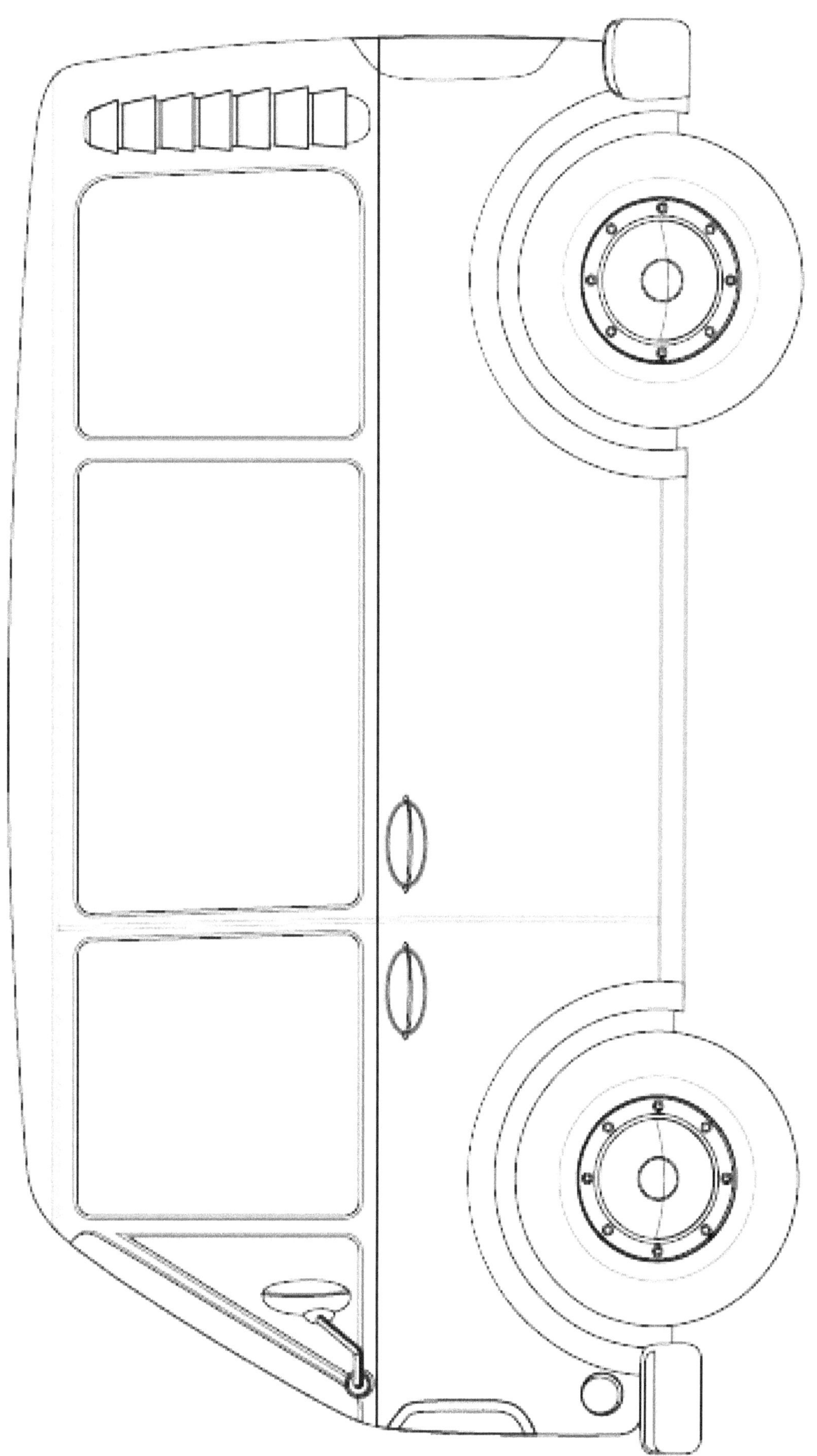

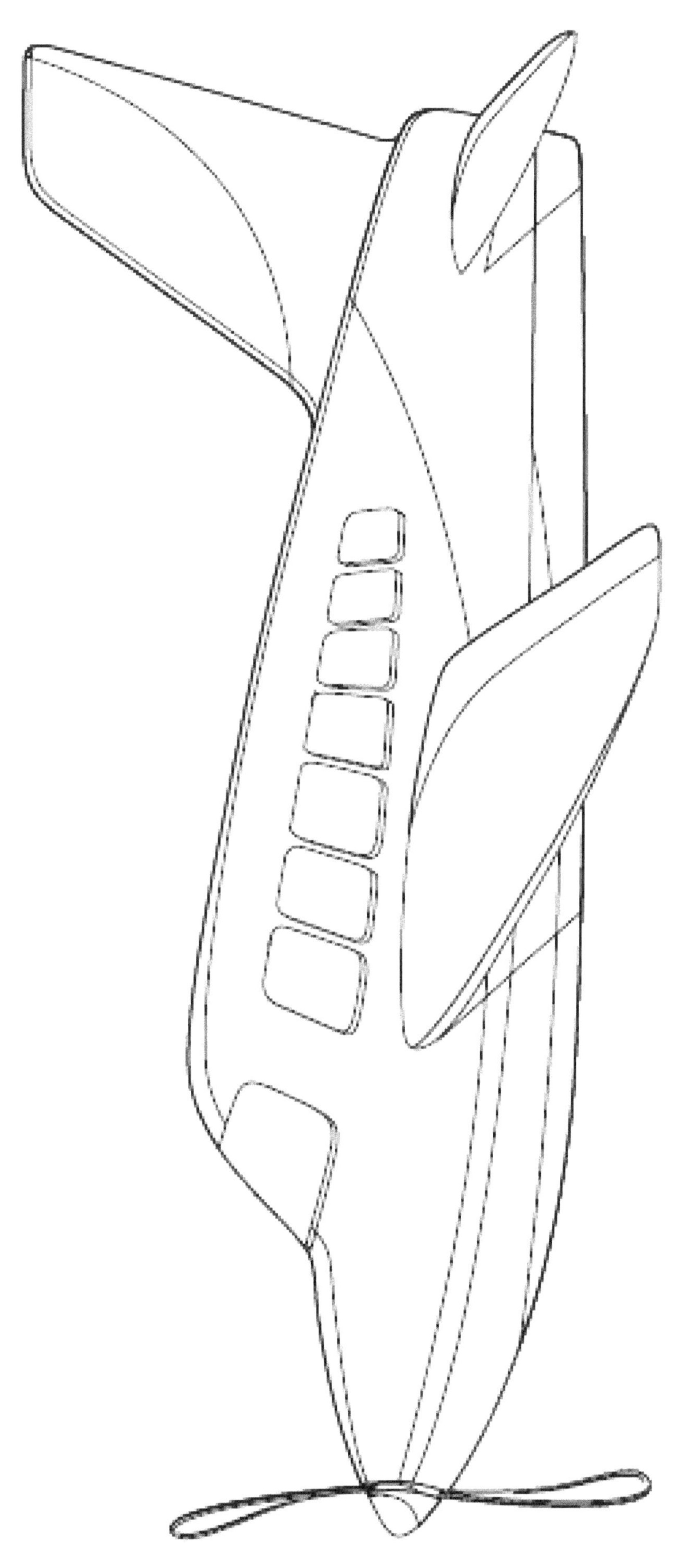

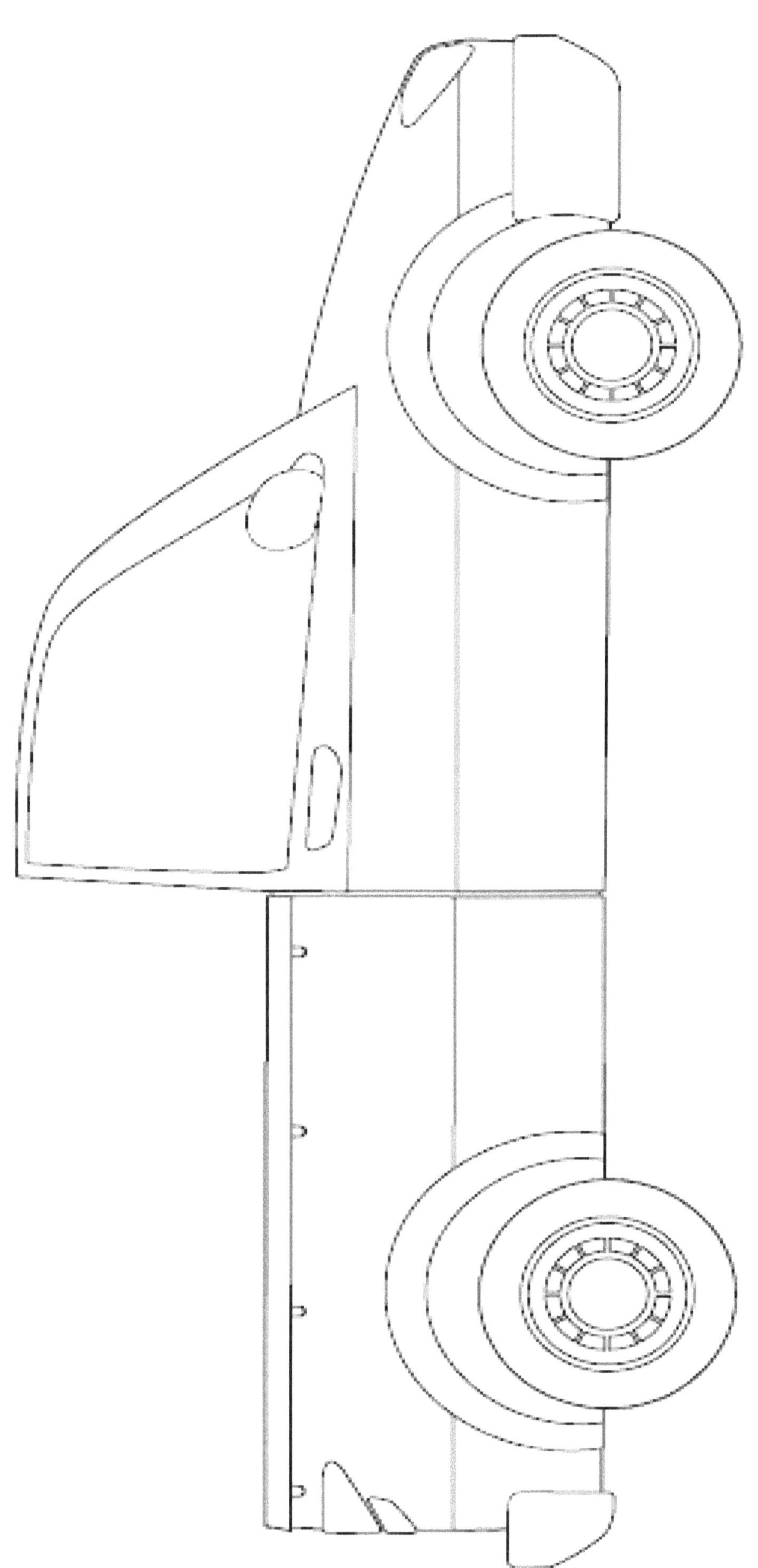

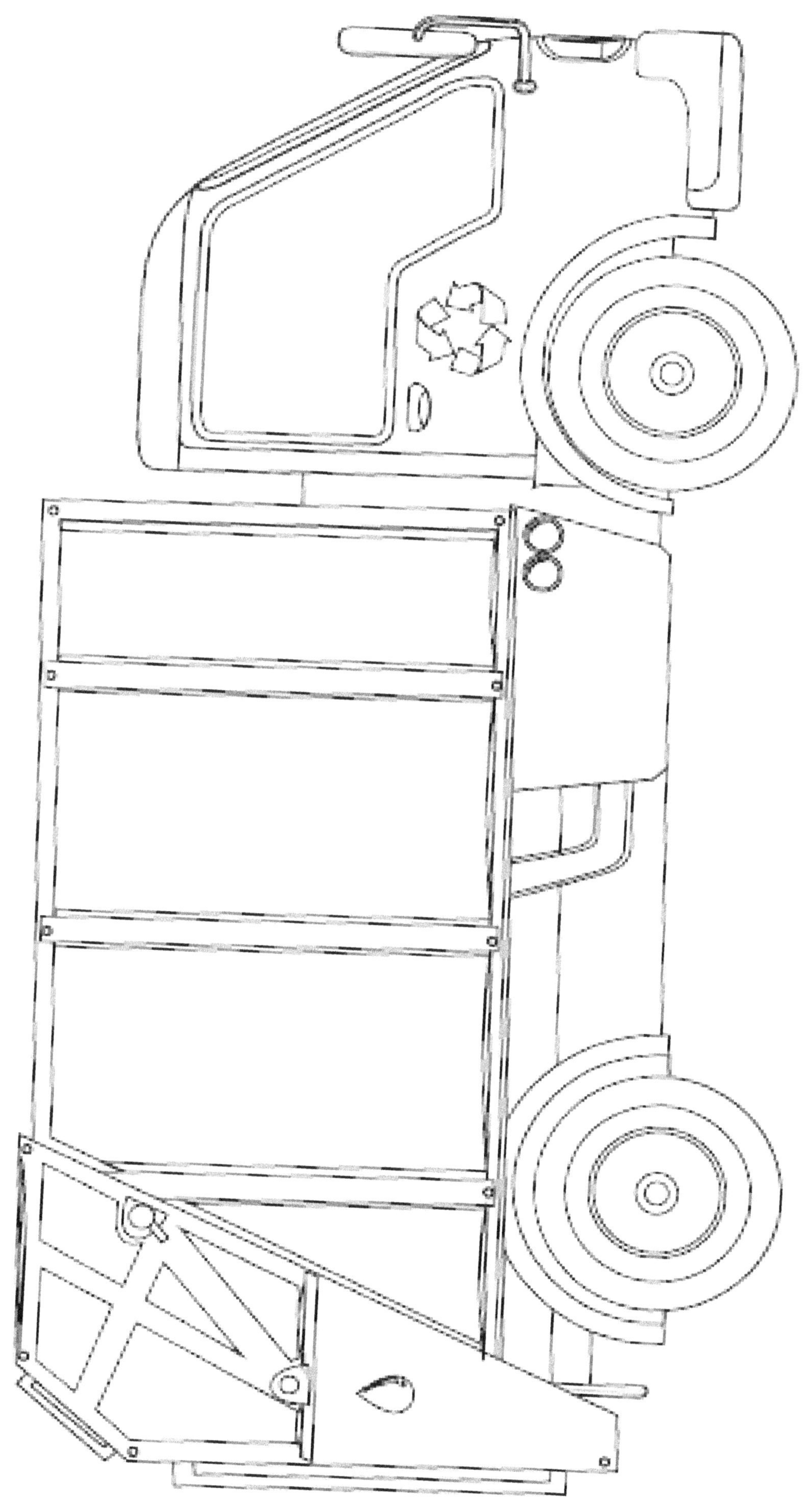

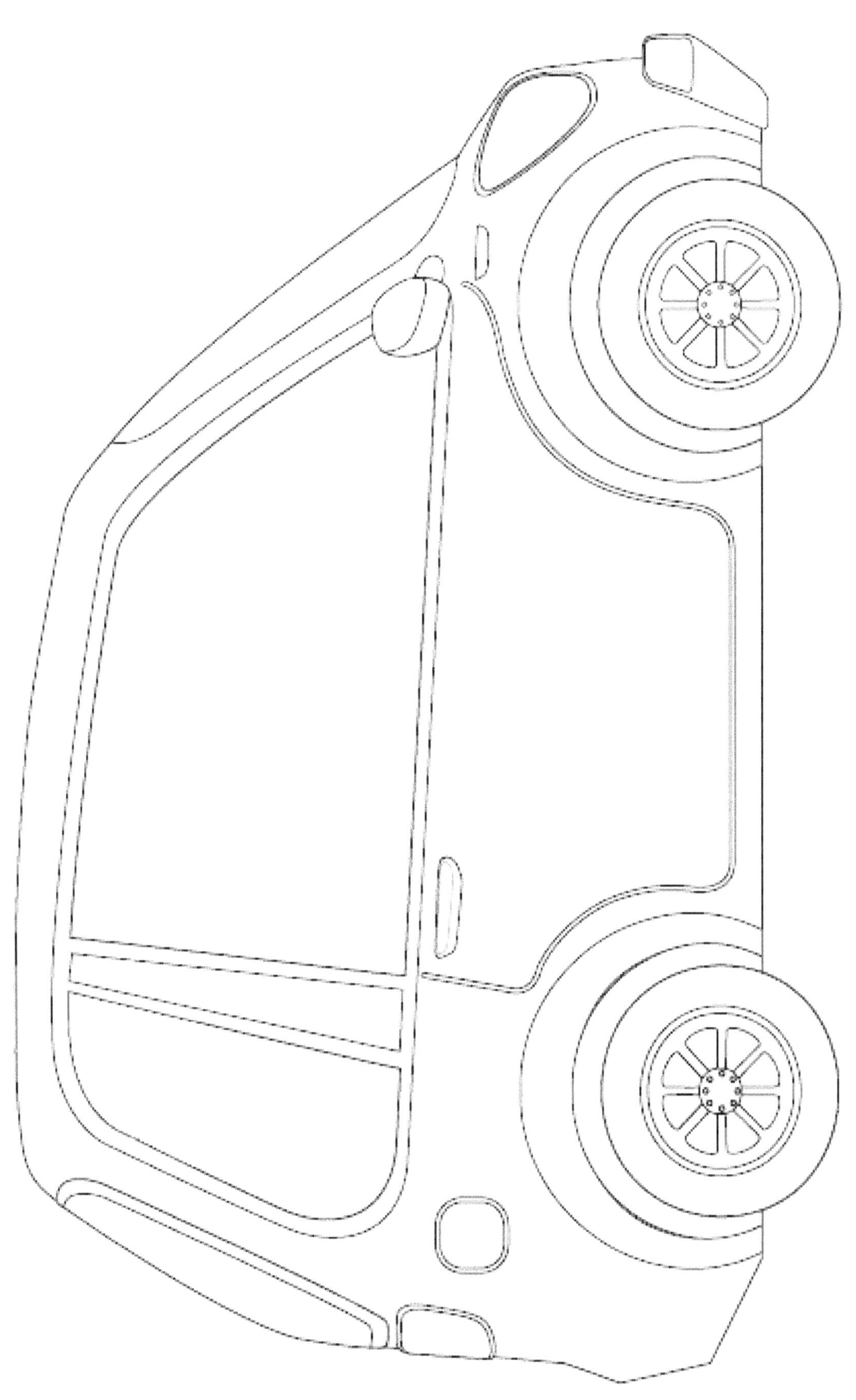

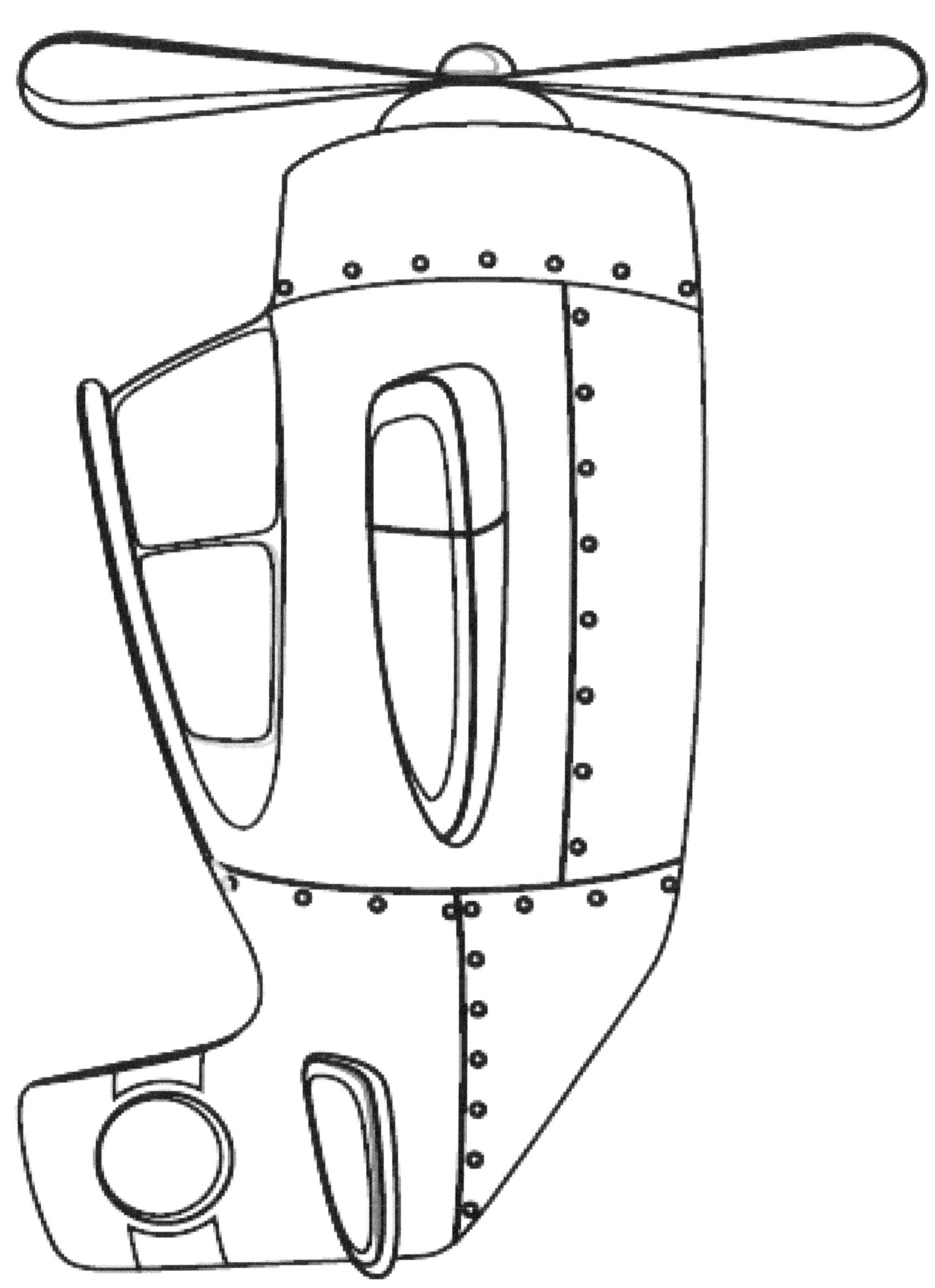

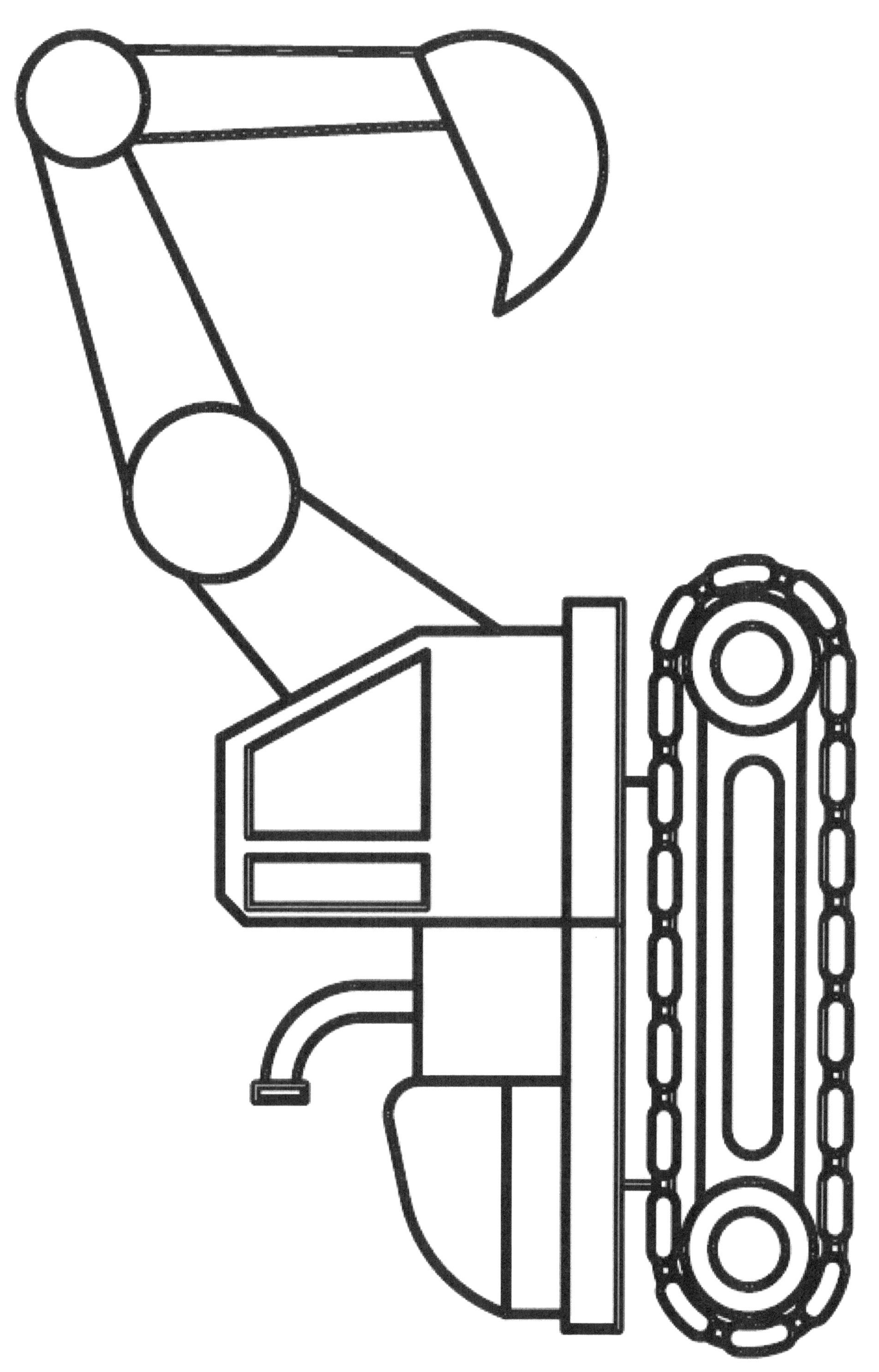

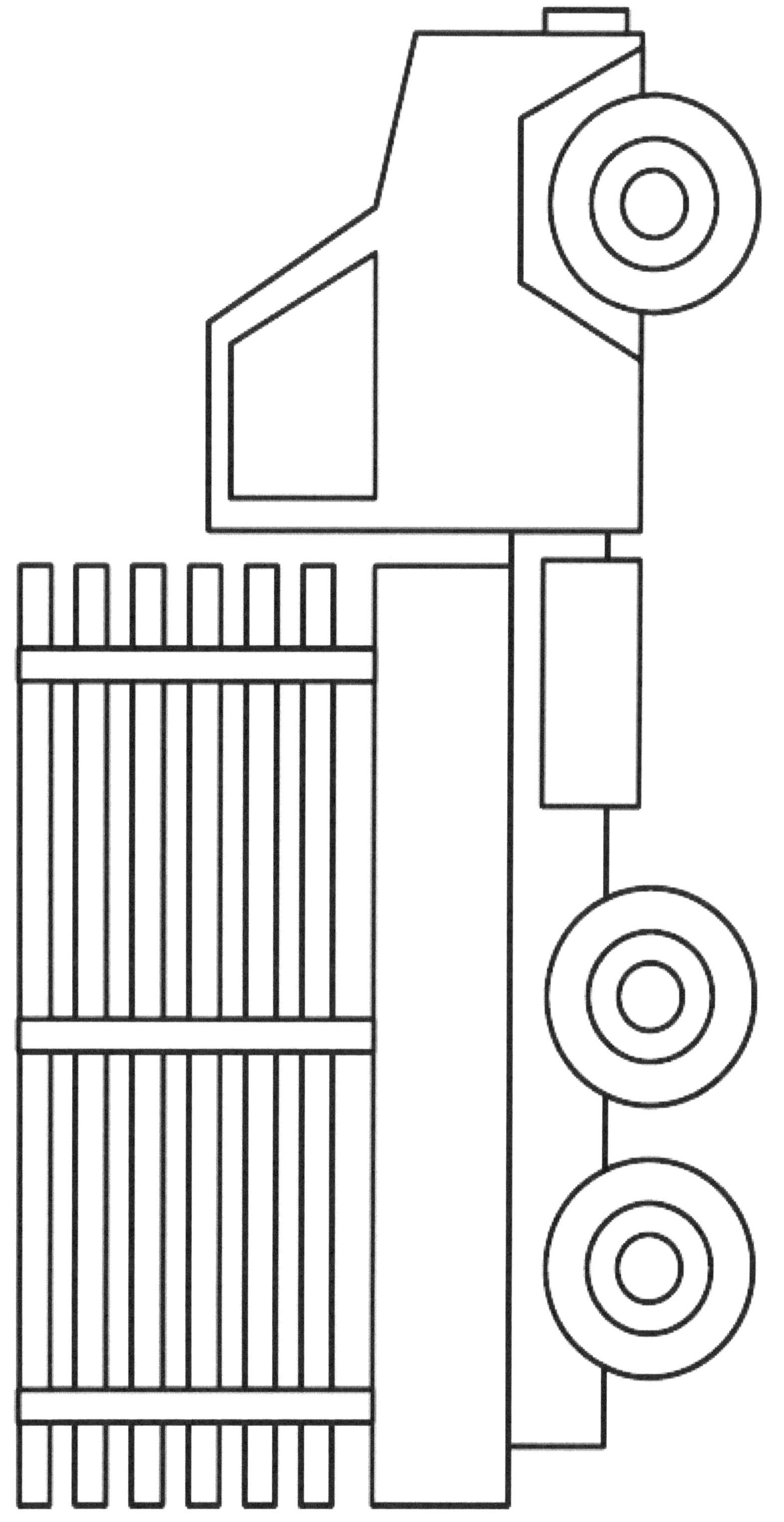

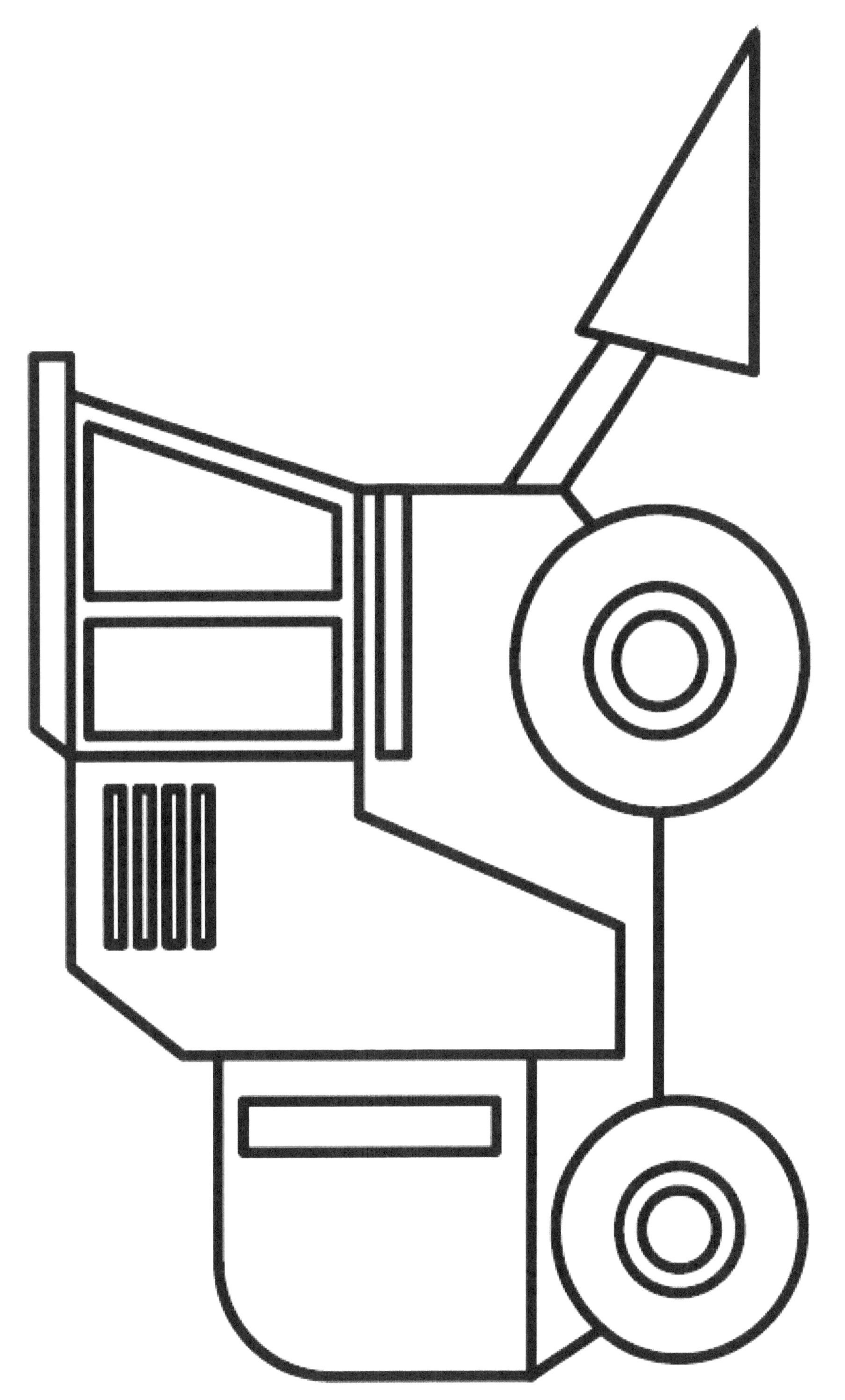